BOTH SIDI

# BOTH SIDES NOW

## Ecclesiastes and the
## Human Condition

PETER BARNES

THE BANNER OF TRUTH TRUST

THE BANNER OF TRUTH TRUST
3 Murrayfield Road, Edinburgh EH12 6EL, UK
P.O. Box 621, Carlisle, PA 17013, USA

\*

ISBN 0 85151 884 2

\*

Unless otherwise stated, Scripture quotations are
from THE HOLY BIBLE, ENGLISH STANDARD VERSION
© 2001 by Crossway Bibles, a division of
Good News Publishers

\*

Typeset in 12 /15 pt Goudy Old Style BT
by Initial Typesetting Services
Edinburgh EH13 9PH

Printed in Great Britain by
Bell & Bain Ltd.,
Glasgow

# Contents

# 1

# Eternity and Madness
# in Our Hearts

David Crosby once quipped that 'Anybody who says he clearly remembers the 1960s obviously wasn't there.'[1] For all its apparently unrestrained hedonism – with sex and dope as substitutes for love and hope – the decade of the 1960s did produce some works of thoughtful reflection. One such example is Joni Mitchell's song *Both Sides Now*, which contains the lines:

> *I've looked at life from both sides now,*
> *From win and lose and still somehow,*
> *It's life's illusions I recall;*
> *I really don't know life at all.*

The song evokes something of the same mood and ethos as the book of Ecclesiastes, found in the Old Testament of the Christian Scriptures. Life is investigated from both sides, yet still remains strangely elusive and unsatisfying. Chesterton once observed that 'The mystery of life is the plainest part of

---

[1] Cited in Steve Farrar, *Point Man* (Oregon: Multnomah, 1990), p. 49.

it.'[2] We seek for happiness and meaning, but they are not easy to find. The answer to this life does not seem to come from within this life. It promises more than it can deliver, and seems to look beyond itself.

What are we as human beings? What is the human condition? How are we to understand ourselves and this life in which we find ourselves? We are indeed strange beings. Ecclesiastes says that we have eternity in our hearts (*Eccles.* 3:11), but it also says that we have madness in our hearts (*Eccles.* 9:3). How can these two, apparently contradictory, things be true?

Human beings are special, but limited. Within each one of us there is a concept of perfection but also a concept of evil. Robert Burns led an immoral life, and in his *A Prayer in the Prospect of Death* tried to ask for forgiveness from God, and yet also tried to blame his sad predicament on his God-given genes:

> *Thou know'st that Thou hast formed me*
> *With passions wild and strong;*
> *And listening to their witching voice*
> *Has often led me wrong.*

We all think of doing better than we actually manage to do. We are tempted to blame our environment or our family that this is so, but the truth is that there is something wrong deep down within each of us. We carry about a kind of madness.

This is an obvious truth that many people choose to deny. In his *Leaves of Grass*, Walt Whitman wrote: *I celebrate myself, and sing to myself.* His philosophy of life was a hollow,

---

[2] Cited in Os Guinness, *Long Journey Home* (Colorado Springs: Waterbrook Press, 2001), p. 2.

complacent one: 'I have never had any particular religious experiences – never felt that I needed to be saved – never felt the need of spiritual regeneration – never had any fear of hell or distrust of the scheme of the universe. I always felt that it was perfectly right and for the best.'[3] This kind of pantheistic optimism was out of place even in the Victorian era; in our era of Auschwitz, the Gulag Archipelago and international terrorism, it ought to arouse a mixture of sympathy and derision.

We also know of God yet we cannot fathom him. We know that he is eternal and perfect, but that is precisely our problem. We know more than the dog knows, but by ourselves we can no more achieve eternity and perfection than the dog can. We are moral beings who fall short of moral perfection. We know what we ought to be but we are not what we ought to be. C. S. Lewis has rightly identified two facts as the foundations of all clear thinking: 'First, that human beings, all over the earth, have this curious idea that they ought to behave in a certain way, and cannot really get rid of it. Secondly, that they do not in fact behave that way.'[4]

We seem to have something in common with the angels and something in common with the cockroach. So here we are, with eternity and madness in our hearts. That is said of you and me, and everybody who has ever lived or will live in this world. In seventeenth-century France the great scientist and Christian thinker, Blaise Pascal, pondered this truth and recorded in his *Pensées*: 'What sort of freak then is man! How

---

[3] Cited in Ruth Tucker, *Walking Away from Faith* (Illinois: IVP, 2002), p. 50.

[4] C. S. Lewis, *Mere Christianity*, 1952 (reprinted Glasgow: Fontana, 1975), p. 19.

novel, how monstrous, how chaotic, how paradoxical, how prodigious! Judge of all things, feeble earthworm, repository of truth, sink of doubt and error, glory and refuse of the universe!'[5] Thus it is that man transcends man.

Unless we can fathom something of the double-sided character of this world, we are doomed never to understand it. The creation – indeed, all of life as we experience it – has two sides. It is full of the goodness of the Lord (*Psa.* 33:5). Gerard Manley Hopkins wrote: 'The world is charged with the grandeur of God.' The world points to God; the goodness and beauty of the creation points to a Creator who is both all-powerful and all-good. Francis of Assisi wrote, in a hymn put together and revised by William Henry Draper in the 1920s:

> *Dear mother earth who day by day*
> *Unfoldest blessings on our way,*
> *O Praise Him, Alleluia!*
> *The flowers and fruits that in thee grow,*
> *Let them His glory also show.*

That is one side – there are flowers and beautiful sunsets. The creation sings of its Creator (*Psa.* 19:1–6).

The other side is that nature is, as Tennyson put it, 'red in tooth and claw'. The female praying mantis eats her mate. Nature is not always beautiful. It threatens us, and can be highly dangerous. At times it is ugly and chaotic. The forces of nature have taken a heavy toll of human life. There are wolves as well as lambs, weeds as well as roses, sharks as well as kittens, and wild tornadoes as well as gentle breezes. There is death and life, ugliness and beauty, the decay of autumn

---

[5] Blaise Pascal, *Pensées* (Harmondsworth: Penguin, reprinted 1973), p. 64.

and the renewal of spring. Alongside the grandeur and majesty of mountain ranges and the tenderness of budding flowers, there are floods, storms, droughts, plagues and other disasters. Something is wonderfully good about the world and something is also terribly wrong about it.

The creation was subjected to 'futility' (*Rom.* 8:20). The New International Version translates this as 'frustration'. So there is something radically wrong, not only within my soul and yours, but outside too. When madness took over Adam's soul in his rebellion against God, Adam himself was cursed, but so too was the creation. God declared: 'Cursed is the ground because of you.' He went on to speak of Adam's battling with thorns and thistles, and his eating his bread in the sweat of his face (*Gen.* 3:17–19a; see too *Psa.* 107:33–34). The entry of sin into the world affected the whole creation, and not just human beings.

Life is good because it comes from God who is good, but life is fallen because of the entry of sin into the world. Those who reject this double-sided view of life and the creation fall into one error or another. They might place all their hopes in the created world, and virtually worship it as Mother Nature. This is the error of much of the modern Green Movement, but the world has never lacked those who worshipped the creature rather than the Creator. More mystical evolutionists pin their hopes on the vague belief that somehow the world will evolve into a higher state, given enough time and the right ingredients from chance. Others have rejected the world as demonic, and sought to flee from it. In the ancient world, such people were known as Gnostics. In extreme versions of this philosophy, it was thought that the devil had created the world.

The world, however, gives evidence that it ought neither to be worshipped nor despised. The creation was subjected to

[5]

futility but also in hope (*Rom.* 8:20). Vanity, vanity, but yet not all is vanity; there is also hope. Good things are in store for the creation. It awaits – literally, it 'stretches the neck and cranes forward' – for the deliverance (*Rom.* 8:19). Now the creation groans: it, as it were, sets up 'a grand symphony of sighs', as John Murray puts it. Yet these groans are not death pangs; they are birth pangs. The creation knows both futility and hope, but hope will win out. John Milton wrote *Paradise Lost* but he also wrote *Paradise Regained.* The death, decay and disorder that are an obvious part of the present creation will be swept aside. This will not be as a result of natural selection but of God's plan.

Then, and only then, shall all the frustrations, vanity, and meaninglessness of this life be swept up in the fulfilment of the Christian hope of the resurrection of the body and the final defeat of sin and death. Before you discard this as outmoded religious thinking, ponder what the book of Ecclesiastes has said about the eternity and madness in our hearts. Does this not fit in with our experience of life here on earth? Nature itself testifies to this truth. It has all the hallmarks of being originally good, but now exhibits much that is destructive and even dangerous.

This may not be the sort of message which you wanted to hear. By natural inclination, we would rather be left alone, and not faced with these matters. We tend to live today by distractions. Sport or academia, vandalism or corporate success, being a workaholic or dropping out of society – these may all be variations on a theme.

We try to live vicariously via the television. People do not live themselves, but watch other people live – how they fix up backyards, live in houses, or perform outlandish stunts. These seem to be only substitutes for real life. Before we ask whether there is life after death, we might wonder whether there is much life before death. Again, to cite Pascal: 'Since men are unable to cure death, misery, and ignorance, they imagine they can find happiness by not thinking about such things.'[6] But the book of Ecclesiastes seeks to confront us with reality in order that we should ponder the things that really matter.

With good reason, Barry Webb calls Ecclesiastes 'perhaps the most enigmatic book in the Old Testament'.[7] It looks at life from two viewpoints – with God and without God. A key word is 'vanity'. Readers of the King James Version will be familiar with the refrain: 'Vanity of vanities,' says the Preacher, 'vanity of vanities! All is vanity' (*Eccles.* 1:2). The word for 'vanity' might also be rendered 'futility' or even 'meaninglessness', as we find in the New International Version. Tremper Longman III translates it as 'completely meaningless'.[8] O. Palmer Robertson's suggestion is 'Frustration of frustrations, frustration of frustrations, all is frustration.'[9] Perhaps we could even translate it as 'breath', 'vapour', or 'mist', since it refers to what is transient or ephemeral, and, in the end, profitless.

This word 'vanity' or 'transience' or 'meaninglessness' is found throughout Eccesiastes – about 36 times, in fact. The Preacher looks at life from various angles. To know the truth, we have to face up to error. What point is there in getting up

---

[6] Blaise Pascal, *Pensées* p. 66.

[7] Barry G. Webb, *Five Festal Garments* (Leicester: Apollos, 2000), p. 83.

[8] Tremper Longman III, *The Book of Ecclesiastes* (Michigan: Eerdmans, 1998), pp. 61–65.

[9] O. Palmer Robertson, *Coming Home to God* (Darlington: Evangelical Press, 2003), p. 13.

in the morning, eating our cornflakes, going to work, coming home, and watching television, day after day until finally it all comes to an end? Do we then all graduate to a big mansion in the sky to eat cornflakes and watch television for all eternity? Or do we rot in our graves, and fade from living memory? Is that what it is all about?

The author of the book of Ecclesiastes is identified as the Preacher (Qoheleth). He is also called the son of David, king in Jerusalem (*Eccles.* 1:1) – hence the widespread and quite likely belief that it was Solomon. Solomon had gained a reputation for being the wisest of men (*1 Kings* 3–4; *Prov.* 1:1; 10:1; 25:1), but descended into idolatry and folly when he took to himself a harem of seven hundred wives and three hundred concubines, many of whom worshipped other gods (*1 Kings* 11:1–11). Ecclesiastes may well be the record of his struggle back to faith – something like Augustine's *Confessions* and *Retractions* rolled into one work.

There is no tight formal structure to the book. It is a somewhat rambling work where the Preacher looks at life from both sides. Ecclesiastes does provide us ultimately with an answer. As Michael Eaton puts it: 'It defends the life of faith in a generous God by pointing to the grimness of the alternative.'[10] Yet, as Graeme Goldsworthy has pointed out,[11] Qoheleth is not simply opposing secularism. There are, in fact, no glib answers, not even religious ones. If blatant secular atheism is an example of vanity, so too is trite religiosity.

---

[10] Michael Eaton, *Ecclesiastes* (Leicester: IVP, 1983), p. 44.
[11] Graeme Goldsworthy, *Gospel and Wisdom* (Devon: Paternoster, 1987), p. 113.

There is a profound sense of alienation in the human soul. The Negro spiritual laments the human condition:

*Sometimes I feel like a motherless child –*
*A long way from home.*

It is often thought that such songs apply to the harsh realities endured by the slaves on the cotton plantations in the southern states of nineteenth-century America, but they also apply to the highly-paid media executive in a swish apartment. The truth is that we feel homesick even at home. The world promises more than it delivers; the title page is better than the contents.

In the dark days of World War II, Hugh Kingsmill made the perceptive observation that 'Most of the avoidable suffering in life springs from our attempts to escape the un-avoidable suffering inherent in the fragmentary nature of our present existence. We expect immortal satisfactions from mortal conditions, and lasting and perfect happiness in the midst of universal change.'[12] He was almost saying that human beings need the realistic outlook of the book of Ecclesiastes if they are to know anything of true happiness – or at least avoid misery born of naivety.

Qoheleth looks at life through melancholy eyes: 'What does man gain by all the toil at which he toils under the sun? A generation goes, and a generation comes, but the earth remains forever' (*Eccles.* 1:3–4). We are constantly being exhorted to make a difference, but the reality is that the world hardly seems much different because we have heeded the alarm clock, eaten breakfast, said good-bye to the family,

---

[12] Hugh Kingsmill, *The Poisoned Crown* (London: Eyre & Spottiswoode, 1944), p. 7.

boarded the train, put in our eight hours' work, returned home, all in order to flop down in front of the television set. There is activity and apparent change, but no sense of getting anywhere. The world at large remains much the same.

Strange, isn't it, how life seems to be getting more comfortable and more hectic at the same time? It is all rather like running on a treadmill, with no satisfaction, no sense of progressing towards a goal: 'All things are full of weariness; a man cannot utter it; the eye is not satisfied with seeing, nor the ear filled with hearing' (*Eccles.* 1:8). In the eighteenth century a whimsical Horace Walpole wrote in his journal: 'Everything seems to be at sea, except the Fleet.'

We move to and fro, but there seems to be no obvious destination. This invariably leads to monotony and frustration. No breakthrough is made; no lasting impressions are left. 'What has been is what will be, and what has been done is what will be done, and there is nothing new under the sun. Is there a thing of which it is said, "See, this is new"? It has been already in the ages before us. There is no remembrance of former things, nor will there be any remembrance of later things yet to be among those who come after' (*Eccles.* 1:9–11). As Malcolm Muggeridge said: 'All new news is old news happening to new people.'[13]

These are melancholy sentiments, but Qoheleth is hardly alone in feeling this way. Gaius Petronius Arbiter – one of whose anagrams is 'a pure sour biting satire' – was supposed to have been the Pro-Consul in Bithynia about A.D. 65 when he recorded: 'Every time we were beginning to form teams we would be reorganized . . . I was to learn later in life that we

---

[13] Cited in R. Zacharias, *Deliver Us From Evil* (Dallas: Word, 1996), p. 130.

[10]

tend to meet every situation in life by reorganizing, and a wonderful method it can be for creating the illusion of progress while producing confusion, inefficiency and demoralization.' Alas, this insightful comment is not genuine, but the sentiments expressed have been proved valid down through the ages. Today there are countless government departments, educational institutions, and media outlets that operate on the same principle. Names are changed, new letterheads are ordered, legislation is passed, and motions are carried – all in the name of 'reform', and all to disguise the fact that nothing of substance has changed.

Before he became a Christian, Augustine of Hippo in North Africa, envied a beggar who was happy because he had been given a good meal. Consumed by his own ambitions and lusts, Augustine knew no such happiness. He saw that 'the world is drunk with the invisible wine of its own perverted, earthbound will'.[14] Augustine himself yearned for perfection and freedom, but found only sin and bondage.

Many centuries later, the great Russian novelist Leo Tolstoy went through a spiritual crisis, and asked himself: 'What is life for? To die? To kill myself at once? No, I am afraid. To wait for death till it comes? I fear that even more. Then I must live. But what for? In order to die? And I could not escape that circle. I took up the book, read, and forgot myself for a moment, but then again, the same question and the same horror. I lay down and closed my eyes. It was worse still.'[15]

[14] Augustine, *Confessions* trans. by R. S. Pine-Coffin, (Harmondsworth: Penguin, 1973), II,3.

[15] Cited in Colin Chapman, *The Case for Christianity* (Herts: Lion, 1981), p. 15.

Tolstoy was not down and out when he wrote those words. Rather, he was at the height of his powers. He had all that most human beings wish for. He had fame, money, a wife and family, achievements, prestige, influence – virtually everything. All the popular psychologists of today would say that his self-esteem should have been healthy, and destined for yet more growth. Yet nothing satisfied him. It was not failure that had left him feeling empty and alienated, but success. People cannot bear to think too deeply about the human condition, and they resent being confronted with it. That is why the worst punishment of all is solitary confinement. An hour by ourselves in our own room is more than most of us can bear.

What about you? Can you answer Tolstoy's questions? What about your family and friends? Are you not somewhat reluctant and afraid even to ask these questions? What is life like without God? And what is life like with God? Perhaps you would like to discuss this at a more convenient time. That, of course, is just a brush off, a delaying tactic. These questions are never convenient – but they are crucial.

Friedrich Nietzsche proclaimed that God is dead, and therefore everything is permissible. He thought that was a wonderfully liberating thought. Human beings could finally do whatever they liked. With no lawgiver, there can be no absolute law. Fyodor Dostoyevsky also thought that if God is dead, everything is permissible. But he considered that if people did whatever they liked, the result would be brutality, tyranny, immorality, and decay. Who was right? Nietzsche or Dostoyevsky?

What is life like apart from God? With God, what is our morality? Why do we think that we are obliged to do some things and not others, and that this is not just a result of self-interest but duty. Without God, what is our morality? How do we decide how to live? With God, what is the meaning of life? Without God, is there any meaning? Does our mortality affect the way we think and live? Do we rise from our graves to be judged by the God who made us, or do we only fertilize the soil and feed the worms?

The wild French poet, Arthur Rimbaud, declared that 'Life is a farce that all must go through.' The English painter, Francis Bacon, was of the same ilk: 'Man now realizes that he is an accident, that he is a completely futile being, that he has to play out the game without reason.'[16] So many people look at the world, and find no meaning, and leave it at that. Another night of television, another round of golf, another day with the family, another newspaper to read – and finally – afar off, one hopes – the end. But the end of what? And the beginning of what? Are we just, as the song goes, 'forever blowing bubbles'?

Qoheleth looked at the world, and saw much vanity, but then lifted his eyes to another world. He knew why Joseph Hall would pray in the seventeenth century: 'The continuance, even of the best things, cloyeth and wearieth: there is nothing but Thyself, wherein there is not satiety.'[17] That is phrased in what seems to be quaint language to us, but the vital truth is that nothing on this earth fully satisfies. In fact, everything ultimately proves distasteful to us. The more we are gratified, the less we are satisfied. Too much ice-cream or chocolate and we become sick, too much money and we suspect it owns us rather than the other way around, too much pleasure and we become bored with it all.

---

[16] Cited in Colin Chapman, *The Case for Christianity* p. 220.
[17] Joseph Hall (1574–1656), from his *Contemplations* (reprinted Michigan: Baptist Book Trust, 1976), p. 2.

Is it all vanity? Does the brevity of life mean that it is doomed to perpetual meaninglessness? We are lonely, we are vulnerable and we are finite. Is that all there is to life? It is tough, rather pointless, and then we die. Can we say anything more than that? Are there avenues worth pursuing?

# 2

# Fulfilment in Wisdom

Perhaps you remain unconvinced by what you see as the negativity of the first chapter. After all, it is one of the clichés of modern life that it is compulsory to be positive rather than negative. You might be one who responds to this by saying: 'I am busy with my university course, and I am finding fulfilment there. You are trying to make me feel miserable when in fact I am enjoying my studies.' It is a common enough sentiment, one that often pleases the parents of such students.

Qoheleth too applied his heart to seek and to search out by wisdom all that is done under heaven. Alas, he found the whole exercise to be 'an unhappy business' (*Eccles.* 1:12–13). The Preacher is not saying that he went to university, spent all his time in the bars and coffee shops, and failed. No, he is saying something far more depressing than that. He is saying that he worked hard at acquiring wisdom, and still found no point to it. It was not failure but success that brought dissatisfaction. Qoheleth succeeded: 'I said in my heart, "I have acquired great wisdom, surpassing all who were over Jerusalem before me, and my heart has had great experience of wisdom and knowledge"' (*Eccles.* 1:16).

Yet where did it lead? Aristotle and Descartes thought that the intellect was the key to understanding humanity and life.

But Qoheleth says that the pursuit of wisdom led nowhere. Nothing changes. Wisdom makes a minimal impact on a flawed world: 'I applied my heart to know wisdom and to know madness and folly. I perceived that this also is but a striving after wind. For in much wisdom is much vexation, and he who increases knowledge increases sorrow' (*Eccles.* 1:17–18). Moffatt translates verse 18 as 'The more you understand, the more you ache.' Intelligent people who think and read widely tend to be cynical and pessimistic. The pursuit of wisdom apart from God has that effect on us.

At times Qoheleth points to a breakthrough: 'So I turned to consider wisdom and madness and folly. For what can the man do who comes after the king? Only what has already been done. Then I saw that there is more gain in wisdom than in folly, as there is more gain in light than in darkness' (*Eccles.* 2:12–13). It is obviously true that some things are better than others, and that all options are not equally valid or invalid.

Qoheleth struggles with what it is all about. It is a controversial passage, but in Ecclesiastes 7:16–17 he seems to take refuge in a middle of the road approach: 'Be not overly righteous, and do not make yourself too wise. Why should you destroy yourself? Be not overly wicked, neither be a fool. Why should you die before your time?' Matthew Henry suggests that we can undo a good thing by overdoing it. This is true even of religion, although it is more accurate to say that piety can easily become contaminated by fanaticism or Pharisaism. Robert Burns was no friend to true Christianity but his mocking satire, *Holy Willie's Prayer*, has a point.[18]

---

[18] See Ian McIntyre, *Dirt and Deity: A Life of Robert Burns* (London: Harper Collins, 1995), pp. 52–55.

Nevertheless, Qoheleth suggests that some things are better than others.

For example, he comes to see that 'a good name is better than precious ointment' (*Eccles.* 7:1a). The Preacher has the sense to observe that a man may accumulate great wealth, possessions, and honour, yet not live to enjoy them (*Eccles.* 6:1–2). Even if he does it may be a case of 'All the toil of man is for his mouth, yet his appetite – the New King James Version has 'soul' – is not satisfied' (*Eccles.* 6:7). Shakespeare referred to appetite as a 'universal wolf'. Wisdom recognizes that it is better to be thought of as a good man rather than as a man who wallows in luxury.

It can also be said that seriousness is better than frivolity: 'It is better to go to the house of mourning than to go to the house of feasting, for this is the end of all mankind, and the living will lay it to heart. Sorrow is better than laughter, for by sadness of face the heart is made glad. The heart of the wise is in the house of mourning, but the heart of fools is in the house of mirth. It is better for a man to hear the rebuke of the wise than to hear the song of fools. For as the crackling of thorns under a pot, so is the laughter of the fools; this also is vanity' (*Eccles.* 7:2–6). The man who never laughs is an unwelcome companion but so too is the man who does nothing but laugh. Wisdom recognizes that there is a need for seriousness as well as laughter.

Qoheleth also sees that honesty is better than corruption: 'Surely oppression drive the wise into madness, and a bribe corrupts the heart' (*Eccles.* 7:7). Furthermore, patience is better than rashness: 'Better is the end of a thing than its beginning, and the patient in spirit is better than the proud in spirit. Be not quick in your spirit to become angry, for anger lodges in the bosom of fools' (*Eccles.* 7:8–9). Self-control is good; anger is destructive – we need to be quick to hear, slow to speak, and slow to anger, as James says (*James* 1:19–20).

It is wise to recognize that nostalgia is pointless: 'Say not, "Why were the former days better than these?" For it is not from wisdom that you ask this' (*Eccles.* 7:10). It is also wise to recognize, as the Serenity Prayer exhorts us, to know the difference between those things in life that we can change and those that we cannot. Contentment is better than grumbling: 'Consider the work of God: who can make straight what he has made crooked? In the day of prosperity be joyful, and in the day of adversity consider: God has made the one as well as the other, so that man may not find out anything that will be after him' (*Eccles.* 7:13–14).

Wisdom is a worthy thing. It is better than power: 'Wisdom gives strength to the wise man more than ten rulers who are in a city' (*Eccles.* 7:19). And being thick-skinned is better than being thin-skinned: 'Do not take to heart all the things that people say, lest you hear your servant cursing you. Your heart knows that many times you have yourself cursed others' (*Eccles.* 7:21–22). Our own sins of the tongue should make us forgiving towards others. Truly, as Pascal declared: 'I state it as a fact that if all men knew what others say of them behind their backs, there would not be four friends left in the world.'[19]

The advocates of complete honesty are being naïve in this fallen world. We are prone to speak ill of others yet deeply resent it when others speak ill of us. There is a cartoon that portrays a preacher holding forth to his congregation about the need for all the people to be honest with one another. At the end of the service, one man shakes his hand and says:

[19] Blaise Pascal, *Pensées* p. 266.

'That was a lousy sermon.' Those who advocate complete openness had better not be thin-skinned.

It used to be fairly common for older people to utter little proverbs like this – observations on life which were generally true. They provided some insights into what life is about. Everything is not equally valid or useful. The fact that every-thing is flawed does not mean that everything is equally flawed. There are insights into life which help us to walk in the path of practical wisdom.

True enough, wisdom has some worth, but it all falls apart when Qoheleth thinks about death: 'The wise person has his eyes in his head, but the fool walks in darkness. And yet I perceived that the same event happens to all of them. Then I said in my heart, "What happens to the fool will happen to me also. Why then have I been so very wise?" For of the wise as of the fool there is no enduring remembrance, seeing that in the days to come all will have been long forgotten. How the wise dies just like the fool!' (*Eccles.* 2:14–16).

The biggest fool in the world and the wisest man both die, and for the most part are forgotten. Einstein dies and the court jester dies. This life is temporary and its achievements, such as they are, are temporary. I was once sifting through some books in a second-hand bookshop in Melbourne, and found one of my own books, on sale for 30 cents. There is no immortality to be achieved through the pursuit of wisdom.

Wisdom is better than folly but if death ends it all, what is the point? 'So I hated life, because what is done under the sun was grievous to me, for all is vanity and a striving after wind' (*Eccles.* 2:17). 'When I applied my heart to know wisdom, and to see the business that is done on earth, how neither day nor night do one's eyes see sleep, then I saw all the work of God, that man cannot find out the work that is done under the sun. However much man may toil in seeking, he will not find it out. Even though a wise man claims to know, he cannot find it out' (*Eccles.* 8:16–17). Our wisdom is real, but limited (*Eccles.* 7:23–25).

The pursuit of wisdom sounds noble, but in one sense it is like carving statues out of smoke. Douglas Adams, before his death in 2001, wrote that the answer to life is 42![20] Samuel Beckett put it less enigmatically: 'I have nothing to say, and I can only say to what extent I have nothing to say.' Bertrand Russell asserted: 'The world in which we live can be understood as a result of muddle and accident; but if it is the outcome of deliberate purpose, the purpose must have been that of a fiend. For my part, I find accident a less painful and more plausible hypothesis.'[21]

So much thinking and so much writing – and yet the result may only be zero. There is no point at all. Hence we have the theatre of the absurd, Dadaism in art, poetry which simply dredges the subconscious mind in the hope of finding gold, and 'music' which consists of notes randomly thrown together. In the name of reason, we embrace dementia.

'Of making many books there is no end, and much study is a weariness of the flesh' (*Eccles.* 12:12). Anyone who has read sociological or psychological reports can sympathize with Mark Twain's lament: 'The researches of many commentators have already thrown much darkness on this subject, and it is probable that, if they continue, we shall soon know nothing at all about it.'[22] An Australian university in 2003 awarded a

---

[20] In *The Hitchhiker's Guide to the Galaxy.*

[21] Bertrand Russell, *Why I Am Not a Christian* (London; Unwin Books, 1975), p. 73.

[22] Cited in D. A. Carson, *The Gagging of God* (Michigan: Zondervan, 1996), p. 57.

Ph.D. to a student who investigated the so-called spirituality of homosexuality. In the process he took seriously the view that Jesus was a homosexual who was into astrology. Needless to say, his conclusions were well in place before he ever began his research.

Darwin's publicist, Herbert Spencer, illustrates this more than most authors. He wrote more than he ever read, on whatever subject took his fancy, but hardly anyone now bothers to read any of this immense output. The pursuit of wisdom, in and of itself, is just a matter of books, study, the internet, and fatigue. On and on – always another work to read – but where is it all going? So much of it goes nowhere. The wise prove to be less than wise.

Small wonder that Hilaire Belloc complained with such vehemence that 'Of all forms of stupidity the most crass, the most tedious and yet the most exasperating is learned stupidity; a pompous furniture of accumulated facts unrelated by the intelligence. We all know the symptoms. There is the use of a jargon to impress the gaping public and the substitution of specialist unfamiliar terms for plain English. There is the constant respectful allusion by one pedant to this, that and the other pedant, so as to present the whole herd of them as a sort of sacred college.'[23]

Interestingly enough, Belloc made the additional – and very suggestive – comment that 'The Bible has been made a playground, apparently inexhaustible in its resources, for people of this kind.'[24] Somehow wisdom seems unable to stand on its own two feet. Wisdom on its own manages to look quite

[23] Hilaire Belloc, *The Battle Ground* (London: Cassell and Co, 1936), p. 85.
[24] Hilaire Belloc, *The Battle Ground*, p. 85.

foolish, and usually does not even recognize its own predicament. In 1801 Henry Martyn won the highest prize for
mathematics – that of Senior Wrangler – at Cambridge
University. He looked to have a bright future in front of him.
Yet it failed to satisfy him, and he recorded: 'I obtained my
highest wishes, but was surprised to find I had grasped a
shadow.'[25] Leo Tolstoy wrote some of the most powerful novels
ever published, but he came to realize that there was no
salvation in human creativity. In the 1870s he went through a
spiritual crisis, and wrote: 'As for art and poetry – for a long
time I managed to convince myself under the influence of
success and praise, that they were a possible form of activity,
even though death would destroy all, both my work and the
memory of it. Then I realized that this activity was also a lie.'[26]

In the first century A.D., the Apostle Paul, writing after the
world had read the works of some of the world's greatest
philosophers, including Plato, Socrates and Aristotle,
concluded that 'in the wisdom of God, the world did not
know God through wisdom' (*1 Cor.* 1:21). Human wisdom
has its strengths, and is not to be despised, but let us be honest
– it has run aground. Wisdom is hardly to be measured in quiz
show answers. Indeed, it is sobering to recall that the Nazi
propagandist, Josef Goebbels, earned a Ph.D. from the
University of Heidelberg. Herman Goering was musical and
intelligent, and had a slogan in his office which read: 'He who
tortures animals wounds the feelings of the German people.'[27]

---

[25] John Sargent, *The Life and Letters of Henry Martyn* (Edinburgh:
Banner of Truth, reprinted 1985), p. 15.

[26] Henri Troyat, *Tolstoy* (Harmondsworth: Penguin, reprinted 1970),
p. 521.

[27] Mark Bryant, *Private Lives* (London: Cassell & Co, 2001), p. 167.

A high intellect can be accompanied by selfishness, cruelty, indifference, misery – and nobody escapes death. Aristotle's ladder may be higher than mine but that does not mean it reaches heaven. Even if we have grasped all that we can possibly grasp, there is still something crucial that is missing. Augustine in his *Confessions* said that a man may know all scientific facts, yet 'he is not happy unless he knows You [God]; but the man who knows You is happy, even if he knows none of these things.'[28] Pascal too stated that 'Knowledge of physical science will not console me for ignorance of morality in time of affliction, but knowledge of morality will always console me for ignorance of physical science.'[29] This latter testimony is all the more powerful for having come from one of the world's most distinguished scientists.

So often we do not get it right, despite all our hard study. But, even worse, we may study hard and get it right, and think to ourselves: 'So what?' There is still something vital missing. There has to be more to life than getting the mathematics right. One and one make two, and $E=mc^2$, but does knowing these things make me any better equipped to live life or to face death? Bertrand Russell's edict was: 'What science cannot tell us, we cannot know.'[30] On that principle, I cannot know if my wife and children love me, or even if it is good to have a wife and children.

Augustine confessed, even after his conversion to Christ: 'I am in a sorry state, for I do not know what I do not know!'[31]

---

[28] Augustine, *Confessions* V, 4.

[29] Blaise Pascal, *Pensées* p. 36.

[30] Cited in Kathryn Ludwigson, 'Postmodernism: A Declaration of Bankruptcy' in D. S. Dockery (ed), *The Challenge of Postmodernism* (Michigan: Baker, 1997), p. 282.

[31] Augustine, *Confessions* XI, 25.

Wisdom is good, but it is limited. It is understandable why Neil Postman spoke of us as 'informing ourselves to death' – to match our 'amusing ourselves to death'.[32] Einstein helped to invent the atomic bomb, but later expressed the wish that he had become a watchmaker instead!

[32] In a speech given in Stuttgart, Germany on 11 October 1990.

# 3

# Happy Are Those
# Who Pursue Pleasure

'Well, what do you expect?' might be your response, 'I have never met an egghead yet who didn't have trouble tying his shoe-laces and cooking toast. Bertrand Russell pontificated on mathematics and philosophy, but was unable to make himself a cup of tea.[33] Study leads nowhere. Better to go out into life, embrace it, and enjoy it to the full. Study makes for dullness. Life is meant to be lived.' On this principle, perhaps there might be more to be gained from night clubs than from lecture halls.

To some extent, that was Qoheleth's response too, although he wanted to embrace pleasure without letting go of wisdom. Qoheleth writes: 'I said in my heart, "Come now, I will test you with pleasure; enjoy yourself"' (*Eccles.* 2:1). The Preacher indulged himself with everything; he denied himself nothing: 'I searched with my heart how to cheer my body with wine – my heart still guiding me with wisdom – and how to lay hold on folly, till I might see what was good for the children of man to do under heaven during the few days of

---

[33] Paul Johnson, *Intellectuals*, London: Weidenfeld & Nicolson, 1988, p. 202.

their life. I made great works. I built houses and planted vineyards for myself. I made myself gardens and parks, and planted in them all kinds of fruit trees. I made myself pools from which to water the forest of growing trees. I bought male and female slaves, and had slaves who were born in my house. I had also great possessions of herds and flocks, more than any who had been before me in Jerusalem. I also gathered for myself silver and gold and the treasure of kings and provinces. I got singers, both men and women, and concubines, the delight of the children of man. So I became great and surpassed all who were before me in Jerusalem. Also my wisdom remained with me. And whatever my eyes desired I did not keep from them. I kept my heart from no pleasure, for my heart found pleasure in all my toil, and this was my reward for all my toil' (*Eccles.* 2:3–10).

Wine, women, song, building great houses, owning marvellous properties, servants, silver and gold, music, treasures – it is all there. These things would naturally give any man a lot of pleasure. Or would they? Qoheleth found that it palled after a time. The novelty soon wears off, to be replaced by an urge for a yet greater novelty. And so it went on. It was mad and useless vanity (*Eccles.* 2:1–2), and at the end all he could write was: 'Then I considered all that my hands had done and the toil I had expended in doing it, and behold, all was vanity and a striving after wind, and there was nothing to be gained under the sun' (*Eccles.* 2:11).

It must be admitted that an aged debauched hedonist is a pathetic figure – Mick Jagger, at sixty, howling *I Can't Get No Satisfaction* is a cause of bemused admiration at best, and considerable embarrassment at worst. Charles Hay, who was to be raised to the bench as Lord Newton, is remembered for his pronouncement: 'Drinking is my occupation, law my amusement.'[34] Such an outlook on life is not unknown in many cultures and in all levels of society.

Yet it should not be thought that God is against pleasure. The Psalmist says of God: 'You make known to me the path of life; in your presence there is fullness of joy; at your right hand are pleasures forevermore' (*Psa.* 16:11). The Apostle Paul too says that God 'richly provides us with everything to enjoy' (*1 Tim.* 6:17). While he was in prison, Paul wrote the epistle to the Philippians, in which the word 'joy' is found sixteen times. Dr Martyn Lloyd-Jones calls it 'the most lyrical, the happiest, letter which the Apostle ever wrote'.[35] There is no blessing in simply being miserable.

But pleasure apart from God is a grasping for the wind. In that sense, C. S. Lewis was provocative but correct in saying that we human beings have no right to happiness.[36] Happiness requires something greater than itself for it to have meaning. Pop stars and film stars and media magnates are usually the unhappiest people in the world. Popularity is a phantom. Looking good and feeling good are not to be confused with being good.

The story is told of a man who went to see a doctor in Manchester, England in 1808. The man was sick, frightened by the terror of the world, depressed by his life, unable to find happiness anywhere, and with nothing to live for. He confessed that he was suicidal. The doctor decided that there was nothing physically wrong with the man, so he advised him to lighten up, get out and enjoy himself, and go and see

[34] Ian McIntyre, *Dirt and Deity: A Life of Robert Burns* p. 118.
[35] Martyn Lloyd-Jones, *The Life of Joy: Philippians 1–2*, (London: Hodder & Stoughton, 1993), p. 9.
[36] See C. S. Lewis' essay 'We Have No "Right to Happiness"' in *God in the Dock* (Glasgow: Fount Paperbacks, 1979), pp. 102–108.

Grimaldi the clown in the circus, because he was the funniest man alive. The man looked even more downcast and help-less, and confessed to the doctor: 'I am Grimaldi!'

Grimaldi's experience was by no means unique to him or to his times. Woody Allen spends his life trying to be funny – and usually succeeding better than most. But he has con-fessed that he thinks of suicide every day of his life.[37] We usually learn more from hard times than from parties and feasts. Every funeral is a reminder that our own will come too. There is wisdom in knowing that we cannot simply laugh off the tragedies and the pain of this life.

Ernest Hemingway was one of the twentieth century's most hedonistic characters. He drank to excess, chased women, married four times, gambled, hunted and fished – he did just whatever he wanted to do. Nevertheless, in *The Old Man and the Sea* he tells of how a fisherman hauls in a huge fish after a long struggle, but most of it is devoured by sharks before the fisherman gets the fish to shore. It was the story of his own life – which concluded when he shot himself in the head in 1961.

H. L. Mencken once quipped that 'The problem with life is not that it's a tragedy, but that it's a bore.'[38] There is an ancient inscription in the forum of Timgad that declares: 'To hunt, to bathe, to gamble, to laugh, that is to live.'[39] Some of the verbs might change, but that general approach to life has had many devotees down through the ages. Strangely

[37] Marion Meade, *The Unruly Life of Woody Allen* (London: Phoenix, 2000), p. 35.

[38] Cited in Ravi Zacharias, *Can Man Live Without God?* (Dallas: Word, 1994), p. 88.

[39] F. Van der Meer, *Augustine the Bishop* trans. by B. Battershaw and G. R. Lamb, (New York: Harper Torchbooks, 1961), p. 47.

enough, the West today has more entertainment than it has ever had in all its history – and also more boredom. There is a greater risk of its boring itself to death than of its blowing itself to smithereens.

One anonymous college student in the United States wrote in a library book on *Existentialism:* 'All we are is cocaine in the wind, man! Far out, yeah, peace, love, hard drugs.'[40] Life dedicated to pleasure and more pleasure descends into boredom, more exotic and perverse titillations, and finally incoherence. We have the best technology that any civilization has ever produced, yet communication is at a low ebb. We have a thriving entertainment industry, yet the listlessness remains.

Timothy Leary preached that drugs would aid one's sex life, but his second marriage broke down on the honeymoon. Norman Mailer married Marilyn Monroe but the result was not that they lived happily ever after. Mailer in fact married six times. John Maynard Keynes and the Bloomsbury Set of fellow homosexuals like E. M. Forster and Lytton Strachey lived the high life of unrestricted pleasure in the years between the two world wars. Looking back on it, Keynes wrote: 'We repudiated all versions of the Doctrine of Original Sin . . . We were not aware that civilization was a thin and precarious crust erected by the personality and the will of very few, and only maintained by rules and conventions skilfully put across and guilefully preserved. We had no respect for traditional wisdom or the restraints of custom. We lacked reverence . . . for everything and everyone.'[41] The

---

[40] Dave Breese, *Seven Men Who Rule the World from the Grave* (Chicago: Moody, 1990), p. 217.

[41] Cited by Max Teichman in *News Weekly* 5 April 2003, p. 23.

result was not paradise, but what Robert Bork has called 'slouching towards Gomorrah'.[42] The pursuit of pleasure without boundaries ends up in misery without boundaries.

Friedrich Nietzsche once commented, in his own incisive and extreme way: 'I fear we are not rid of God because we still have faith in grammar.'[43] The order in the world implies that there is a Mind behind the order. Order is not in the habit of magically appearing from random disorder. With Postmodernism, however, we have seen a concerted attack on common sense, reason, coherence, and grammar. Michel Foucault was one of the leading proponents of this Postmodernist charge. He asserted that every assertion of knowledge is only an act of power. But, as the old Arab proverb says, to defy reality is to spit into the wind. Foucault lived what he thought was a liberated homosexual lifestyle and experimented with hallucinogenic drugs, before dying of AIDS. The pleasure house became a kind of prison house.

Has that not been your experience? There is the party, the night club, the social life, but also the emptiness, and the hunger for something though you hardly know what. Even music, which transports you out of this world for a time, palls after a while and you need a break from it. No pleasure in this world satisfies deep down, does it? The novelty wears off, the exhilaration palls, and the thrill becomes a kind of drudgery, even bondage. We all end up with the question of Sir Bob Geldof who, in the midst of all his musical, charitable, and public relations successes, asked himself again and again: 'Is that it?'[44]

[42] See Robert Bork, *Slouching Towards Gomorrah: Modern Liberalism and American Decline* (New York: Regan Books, 1996).

[43] W. Kaufmann (ed), *The Portable Nietzsche* (New York: Viking, 1982), p. 483.

[44] The question became the title of a book he wrote.

Happiness is a strange and elusive thing. In 1851 Allen Francis Gardiner died of starvation while trying to open up the southern tip of South America to the gospel. Three of his six companions had already died. Unable to move and without any strength at all, Gardiner wrote:

> Blessed be my heavenly Father for the many mercies I enjoy: a comfortable bed, no pain or even cravings for hunger, though excessively weak, scarcely able to turn in my bed, at least it is a very great exertion; but I am, by His abounding grace, kept in perfect peace, refreshed with a sense of my Saviour's love and an assurance that all is wisely and mercifully appointed.[45]

Not long after writing those words, Gardiner was dead.

Was he happy? He says that he was. Was he serious? Was he deluded? Perhaps he understood more than we suspect, and he really was happy. When Charles Colson took his grandson to Disneyland in 1987, he noticed that no one seemed happy.[46] Happiness is not easily equated with pleasure, or measured in decibels of laughter. The relentless pursuit of pleasure seeks to solve the problem of boredom, but only adds to it. The pursuit of happiness seems to have led to an epidemic of depression. Life must be more than something we do when we are not watching television.

---

[45] Owen Milton, *Christian Missionaries* (Bryntirion: Evangelical Press of Wales, 1995), p. 97. For a fuller version, see Phyllis Thompson, *An Unquenchable Flame: The Story of Captain Allen Gardiner, Founder of the South American Missionary Society* (London: Hodder & Stoughton and the SAMS, 1983).

[46] Charles Colson with Ellen Santilli Vaughn, *The God of Stones and Spiders* (Illinois: Crossway, 1990), p. 93.

Charles Simeon stated that 'there are but two lessons for the Christian to learn: the one is, to enjoy God in every thing; the other is, to enjoy every thing in God.'[47] Until you learn that, life's most exuberant expressions of happiness will remain but poignant reminders that there is something far greater and far deeper than the pleasures of this world.

[47] Hugh Evan Hopkins, *Charles Simeon of Cambridge* (London: Hodder and Stoughton, 1977), p. 203.

# 4

# Work at It

Maybe the best thing to do is simply not to think about these things, nor abandon oneself to pleasure. Perhaps the best thing to do is just to beaver away at what you are doing. Work can give meaning to life. The World Fair will stand when Disneyland has fallen. So Qoheleth took to hard work to solve his angst. 'Work is worship,' said Thomas Carlyle. At any rate, it can appear to be a respectable substitute.

Perhaps you have done the same. It takes one's mind off other worries, and enables one to play the role of apparently being important. Far better, surely, to work eighty hours a week than to be left for half an hour alone with your thoughts. Yes, work conveniently distracts the mind from contemplating the human condition. Not much time for the family or friends (except those who can help you climb the ladder at work), and certainly no time to read a book or think about life and death – but perhaps these are the sacrifices that have to be made.

Yet all of Qoheleth's hard work came to nothing: 'I hated all my toil in which I toil under the sun, seeing that I must leave it to the man who will come after me, and who knows whether he will be wise or a fool? Yet he will be master of all for which I toiled and used my wisdom under the sun. This also is vanity. So I turned about and gave my heart up to despair over all the toil of my labours under the sun, because sometimes a person who has toiled with wisdom and knowledge and skill must leave something to be enjoyed by someone who did not toil for it. This also is vanity and a great evil. What has a man from all the toil and striving of heart with which he toils beneath the sun? For all his days are full of sorrow, and his work is a vexation. Even in the night his heart does not rest. This also is vanity' (*Eccles.* 2:18–23).

Hard work may lead to great achievements, but these are fragile and easily undone. Hard work and laziness are not equally futile, but there is something vain and pointless even about the worthwhile things of life. 'Then I saw that all toil and all skill in work come from a man's envy of his neighbour. This also is vanity and a striving after wind. The fool folds his hands and eats his own flesh. Better is a handful of quietness than two hands full of toil and a striving after wind' (*Eccles.* 4:4–6). The workaholic, driven by envy, and the dropout, driven by laziness, are both caught in the futility trap. The answer to the rat race is not dropping out of the rat race. Without God, the empire-builder in the city and the pot smoker in Nimbin are both living meaningless lives. Workaholics – as respectable idolaters – work away, devoting their lives to something that is not God. They press on in the vain hope that they will win the rat race.

Somehow human achievement has a way of undoing itself. We work and strive, but the results never quite match the hopes. Indeed, sometimes the results are quite bizarre. In 1992 Cambridge University conferred an honorary doctorate of literature on the deconstructionist Jacques Derrida who proclaims, in an incomprehensible way, the end of literature!

Early in 2003 Phil Spector gave a rare interview with a journalist.[48] Spector was perhaps the best-known record producer of the time (for the young ones, a record is the sixties' equivalent of a CD). Producing songs for the Righteous Brothers and the Beatles, Spector was also responsible for John Lennon's *Imagine* album, with its wistful attempt to celebrate life without heaven, hell and religion. Tom Wolfe called him the 'first tycoon of teen', but after John Lennon was shot dead in 1980, Spector became a recluse, and remained one until he returned to work briefly in 2002. Then came the news that in early 2003 he had been charged with murder.

No doubt unwittingly, Spector revealed himself as an egotist of the first order, who could not stand anyone to enjoy greater success than he did.

Spector confessed that he wanted immortality through his work, and cited Thomas Jefferson, George Gershwin, and Irving Berlin as men who had succeeded in this. He recalled: 'Those records, when I was making them, they were the greatest love of my life. That's why I never had relationships with anybody that could last.' He paused, then mused sadly: 'That's why I can't figure out why they have so little significance for me today.'

Like the author of Ecclesiastes, Spector lamented that both happiness and unhappiness are temporary. He leaned forward: 'People tell me they idolize me, want to be like me, but I tell them, trust me, you don't want my life. Because it hasn't been a very pleasant life. I've been a very tortured soul. I have not been at peace with myself. I have not been happy.'

[48] *Sydney Morning Herald* 6 February 2003.

Wearing a toupee, Spector was trying to live on in the sixties. He sought for immortality and significance in his work, but found that it could not bear the weight of expectation that he placed on it. For over forty years he visited a psychiatrist in the hope of finding some sanity in his life. Truly, here was one who was 'without hope' (*Eph.* 2:12). Spector was hopelessness personified; he was the message of Ecclesiastes incarnate. It is not only our failures that reveal how weak we are. It can be our successes. Spector climbed to the top of the tree, expecting to eat of its fruits and find satisfaction. Instead, he found there was nothing of lasting significance there. The top of the tree was as bereft of real fruit as the bottom. Work is a god, but it is a god who can neither satisfy nor save.

This world is, as Bunyan called it, the 'City of Destruction'. It has longings for security and significance – for eternity even – but it cannot satisfy them. The wonders of the world end up as ruins. During an election campaign in eighteenth-century England, a political opponent dropped dead, leading Edmund Burke to comment: 'What phantoms we are; and what phantoms we pursue!'[49] We all have these flashes of reality from another world. Alas, we often fail to meditate on them.

It is eternity that makes time significant. It is where we are going that makes what we are doing significant and meaningful. It is so easy to weigh things in the wrong proportions. In Jeremiah's day, God said that the people had committed two sins: 'They have forsaken Me, the spring of living water, and have dug their own cisterns, broken cisterns that cannot hold water' (*Jer.* 2:13).

[49] Cited in D. M. Martyn Lloyd-Jones, *The Puritans* (Edinburgh: Banner of Truth, 1987), pp. 395–396.

Death hangs over everything:

> *Life has no reason,*
> *A struggling through the gloom,*
> *And the senseless end of it*
> *Is the insult of the tomb.*

If death has not been overcome, then that is what it is all about.

Phillip Adams, Australia's resident evangelist for atheism, tells us that death is nothing at all: 'If you want to know what death's like, just think back a few years to before you were born. Death's exactly the same thing.'[50] Armed with such a view of death, it is not surprising that Adams should tell us that the meaning of life can be summed up in the following ditty[51]:

> *As you wander on through life brother*
> *Whatever be your goal*
> *Keep your eye upon the doughnut*
> *And not upon the hole.*

That might reduce some people to tears of gratitude and wonder, but it lacks something when compared to the Damascus Road experience. Adams mocks Christianity, and all he has to put in its place is this banal looking at life's doughnut.

---

[50] Phillip Adams, *Adams Versus God* (Melbourne: Nelson, 1985), p. 182.
[51] Phillip Adams, *Adams Versus God* p. 192.

# 5

# You Can Bank on It

'Ah, but with money, you can buy what you want, live where you like, fill in your days as you please, and answer to nobody. You can be the master of your own destiny.' Such is the dream of every gambler or would-be tycoon. Next time may be the big one. I may scratch the right card, the right coloured balls might fall, the right numbers come up on the screen, the business might suddenly boom, or I might inherit wealth from a relative who conveniently dies. Yes, if only, if only, if only . . .

Qoheleth fell into the same trap, but came to see the futility of it all. 'He who loves money will not be satisfied with money, nor he who loves wealth with his income; this also is vanity. When goods increase, they increase who eat them, and what advantage has their owner but to see them with his eyes? Sweet is the sleep of the labourer, whether he eats little or much, but the full stomach of the rich will not let him sleep. There is a grievous evil that I have seen under the sun: riches were kept by their owner to his hurt, and those riches were lost in a bad venture. And he is father of a son, but he has nothing in his hand. As he came from his mother's womb he shall go again, naked as he came, and shall take nothing for his toil that he may carry away in his hand. This also is a grievous evil: just as he came, so shall he go, and what gain is there to him who toils for the wind? Moreover, all his days he eats in darkness in much vexation and sickness and anger' (*Eccles.* 5:10–17).

Money never seems to satisfy us; the gravy train is always moving. Even if we get what we want, it soon palls. There is no perfect toy, no perfect house, no perfect car. Many lottery winners end up wishing they had never bought a ticket. A woman once approached John Newton, wanting to be congratulated because she had a win in the lottery. Newton was blunt yet compassionate in his reply: 'Madam, as for a friend under temptation, I will pray for you.'[52]

The accumulation of wealth does not bring greater security but less. The world's richest men often live in – to cite Ecclesiastes – darkness, vexation, sickness and anger. Misers lead miserable lives. Howard Hughes was an unhappy recluse for the last decades of his life. Sir J. Paul Getty II, whose father was supposed to be the richest man in the world, became addicted to watching soap operas, particularly *Neighbours*.[53]

The advertisements say that satisfaction is guaranteed, but God says that dissatisfaction is guaranteed. Being rich is not in itself sinful, but it so often works out that the more goods we own, the more they own us. We have everything to live on, but nothing to live for. In 2003 the star English soccer player, David Beckham, transferred from Manchester United to Real Madrid, reportedly for something like £24.5 million. Somehow we know what everything costs but we know the value of nothing. Our own free will imprisons us.

---

[52] Brian Edwards, *Through Many Dangers* (Darlington: Evangelical Press, 2001), p. 299.
[53] *Sydney Morning Herald* 24 April, 2003.

Yet God works in strange ways. As a youth raised in an unbelieving household, Francis Schaeffer was impressed by walking past the city dump each Saturday. He realized that people were devoting their hearts and souls to accumulating things which ended up rusted and discarded at the dump.[54] Ted Turner emerged from all his millions to label Christianity 'a religion for losers'.[55] But what if we are all losers? What if even the winners are losers? What if we gain the whole world and lose our own souls?

The perspective of eternity transforms our view of time in a radical way. As Jonathan Edwards put it: 'If one worm be a little exalted above another, by having more dust, or a bigger dunghill, how much does he make of himself!'[56] We think we are flying through space when we are actually trapped on the ground. We 'lick the dust', to use Pascal's expression, in the vain hope that it is manna from heaven.

Steinbeck in *The Pearl* tells of an Indian who finds a pearl which promises much to his newborn child, but his child is killed when robbers try to steal the pearl. Perspective is everything in life. Light either blinds or enlightens. We own things or they own us. Dietrich Bonhoeffer wrote: 'Earthly possessions dazzle our eyes and delude us into thinking that they can provide security and freedom from anxiety. Yet all the time they are the very source of all anxiety.'[57]

---

[54] Christopher Catherwood, *Five Evangelical Leaders* (London: Hodder & Stoughton, 1984), p. 111.

[55] Cited, for example, in Bernard Goldberg, *Bias* (Washington: Regnery Publishing, 2002), p. 128.

[56] Jonathan Edwards, *Works*, Vol. 1 (Edinburgh: Banner of Truth, reprinted 1976), p. 681.

[57] Charles Ringma (ed), *Seize the Day with Dietrich Bonhoeffer* (Sutherland: Albatross Books, 1991), for May 5.

# 6

# Utopia?

*To dream the impossible dream* – is that a song worth singing? Should we place our hopes in the belief that somehow, given the right conditions, Utopia will be established here on earth? That is a track which has attracted many travellers down through the ages. Often people have sought to implement a reign of peace and goodwill by means of bloodshed and tyranny. Just as often people have been governed by what are mostly good intentions. Alas, we underestimate the power of evil in the human heart. As the Puritan Richard Baxter warned: 'To intend well in doing ill is no rarity.'[58]

Qoheleth saw wickedness where there should have been justice: 'Moreover, I saw under the sun that in the place of justice, even there was wickedness, and in the place of righteousness, even there was wickedness' (*Eccles.* 3:16). The law-courts may be wicked. Jesus spoke too of an unjust judge (*Luke* 18:1). Truly, there is nothing new under the sun! The law can be insane and arbitrary. We can all think of many examples these days. In 1986 in Florida, Joan Andrews pulled

---

[58] Richard Baxter, *The Reformed Pastor*, 1656 (abridged and reprinted Edinburgh: Banner of Truth, 1974), p. 161.

the plug from an unused suction machine in an abortion clinic, and was charged with burglary, malicious mischief, resisting arrest and assault. She received for that heinous crime five years in a maximum security prison. Later that day the same judge gave four years each to two men who were convicted of being accessories to murder.[59]

Nor is this an isolated case. A murderer in Washington state won over $400,000 because a police dog had mangled his foot and so used excessive force in his arrest. Drunks sue bars for selling them drinks. Four kindergarten youngsters were suspended for pretending their fingers were guns and shooting at one another. A part-time masseuse in Australia sued her employer and won $26,000 because she claimed that her clients' complaints had led to her depression, while a woman named Stella won almost three million dollars after scalding herself with coffee at McDonald's. In Los Angeles a thief was awarded $74,000 when his neighbour ran over his hand. The thief was busy stealing the car's hubcaps at the time. Over the years, lawyers, judges and criminals have learned the benefits to be gained by a kind of tacit co-operation.

The distinguished Professor of Law at the University of Colorado, Paul Campos, has written of 'jurismania' – the madness of American law. He points out the obvious – that it is unduly complex, hypertrophied, obsessively perfectionist, and hugely expensive.[60] He cites the saying of Tacitus: 'As

---

[59] See *"You Reject Them, You Reject Me": The Prison Letters of Joan Andrews* edited by Richard Cowden-Guido (Brentwood: Wolgemuth & Wyatt, 1989).

[60] Paul F. Campos, *Jurismania: The Madness of American Law* (New York: Oxford University Press, 1998).

formerly we suffered from crimes, so now we suffer from laws.'[61] Nailing garlic over doorways does not repel vampires, and decade-long appeals, statutes of one thousand pages and regulations of 16,000 pages do nothing for honesty and decency.

What is going on? There is wickedness and a lack of moral proportion in the prisons, but also in the law-courts. Human justice without an anchorage in divine justice easily descends into the realm of the arbitrary – as Franz Kafka so graphically portrayed in *The Trial*. And we all can relate to Mr Bumble in Charles Dickens' *Oliver Twist* who refers to the law as an ass and an idiot.

Utopian hopes have a way of disappearing into smoke. The pop festival at Woodstock in 1969 proclaimed what it thought was peace and love, but when the Isle of Wight tried to repeat the message in 1971, the result was violence and chaos. During the brutal and totalitarian days of the Soviet Union, the news was brought to its citizens by the newspaper *Pravda*. The word actually means 'truth', but the paper only fed the people lies and communist propaganda. Meanwhile in Japan Emperor Hirohito was known as 'Showa', which means 'Enlightened Peace' – again, a most inappropriate title for a war-mongering leader who portrayed himself as a deity. In the Great Leap Forward in China in the 1950s millions died, and the culture went backwards.

The various dictatorships of the proletariat which came to power in the twentieth century invariably turned into dictatorships over the proletariat. The new tyrants were more corrupt and brutal than the tyrants they replaced. After the Berlin Wall came down in 1989, it was found that Erich

---

[61] Paul F. Campos, *Jurismania* p. 3.

Honecker in East Germany owned thirty-two homes, while Nicolae Ceausescu of Romania lived in a palace that was larger than that of King Louis XIV in Versailles.

The quest for peace can be another case in point. It is not uncommon for pacifists to be more vigorous and domineering personalities than recruiting sergeants. In November 1931 there was an international gathering of pacifists in Paris which ended up in acrimonious disputes, to which the police were called. Bertrand Russell used to tell the nations how to live together in peace, but he was utterly unable and unwilling to achieve peace in his own household – four marriages, one wife after another, one affair after another.

All revolutions proclaim messages of high-sounding ideals, but they end up achieving more oppression. The French Revolution proclaimed 'Liberty, equality, and fraternity' but it resulted in tyranny, dictatorship, and mob rule. Beginning with the demand for reason and humanitarianism, it ended up with irrationalism and the Terror. The Tree of Liberty replaced the Cross, and the result was the guillotine. As human beings, we have a way of achieving the opposite of what we are aiming to achieve – rather reminiscent of a bumper sticker I once saw: 'Honk if you love peace and quiet'!

Injustice means that there is no barrier to oppression: 'Again I saw all the oppressions that are done under the sun. And behold, the tears of the oppressed, and they had no one to comfort them! On the side of their oppressors there was power, and there was no one to comfort them. And I thought the dead who are already dead more fortunate than the living who are still alive' (*Eccles.* 4:1–3).

Better off dead, says Qoheleth. The world can be a vicious place. William Cowper lamented:

*My ear is pain'd,*
*My heart is sick, with ev'ry day's report*
*Of wrong and outrage with which earth is fill'd.*

The evil of the world is something that should grieve us – so long as we also grieve over the evil in our own hearts.

Dietrich Bonhoeffer, the Lutheran pastor and theologian, was arrested on 5 April 1942 on suspicion that he was involved in a conspiracy against Hitler. He was taken to Tegel Prison in Berlin. One of the first things he noticed about his prison cell was that a former prisoner had scribbled on the wall, 'In a hundred years it will all be over.'[62] That is one way to cope with injustice. Many have thought it better to capitulate before matters get to that stage. 'Better red than dead' was a slogan during the Cold War of the 1950s. A more realistic one might have been, 'Capitulate to the red and we'll all be dead.' Campaigns for peace may sometimes only indicate a lack of moral backbone, in the same way that ardent militarists may only be hiding a fearful insecurity.

In some societies, injustice has meant concentration camps, secret police and institutionalized brutality. 'If you see in a province the oppression of the poor and the violation of justice and righteousness, do not be amazed at the matter, for the high official is watched by a higher, and there are yet higher ones over them' (*Eccles.* 5:8). There is a pecking order – each one plucks the next one down the line.

If man is just an animal, why not treat him as an animal? 'I said in my heart with regard to the children of man,' writes Qoheleth, 'that God is testing them that they may see that

---

[62] Dietrich Bonhoeffer, *My Soul Finds Rest: Reflections on the Psalms* trans. by Edwin Robertson, (Michigan: Zondervan, 2002), p. 113.

they themselves are but beasts. For what happens to the children of man and what happens to the beasts is the same; as one dies, so dies the other. They all have the same breath, and man has no advantage over the beasts, for all is vanity. All go to one place. All are from the dust, and to dust all return. Who knows whether the spirit of man goes upward and the spirit of the beast goes down into the earth?' (*Eccles.* 3:18–21). What is the difference between Josef Stalin and Francis of Assisi? Or Bill Gates and the cow in the field?

As a family, we once spent half a Saturday morning looking at a flying fox that was hanging upside down in a tree in our backyard. It was all very interesting, until we realized that the animal was dead. We looked at each other with a sense of bemused embarrassment, then went off to do other things. If there is no God, that is how we all end up – not upside down in a tree, necessarily, but dead and rotting.

Peter Singer, a specialist in bioethics, thinks there is nothing wrong with societies that practise abortion, euthanasia, infanticide, and bestiality.[63] This comes from believing that there is no fundamental difference between human beings and animals. If God is dead, so is man. Yet when his mother, Cora Singer, was struck down with Alzheimer's Disease, Professor Singer felt himself unable to live consistently with his own philosophy, and so looked after her rather than remove her by a 'mercy killing'.

Qoheleth rambles through life, making comments on what he observes. He looks at wealth and wisdom, at human attempts at justice, at what one might expect out of life but usually does not get. And he especially notes that death hovers over everything. What is the point of success and of

---

[63] See Gordon Preece (ed), *Rethinking Peter Singer* (Illinois: IVP, 2002).

goodness if death ends it all? Genesis 3 is behind all of life – the world was created good, but it has fallen. Charles Bridges comments: 'So degraded is man, that he cannot understand his own degradation.'[64] The next step upwards is Hugh Kingsmill's insight that 'Disillusionment is the result of discovering that other people are as egotistical as oneself.'[65] We have eternity and madness in our hearts. We know God and we know sin.

It is not that we are born good, but then corrupted by society. There is something deeply perverse in each of us. John Dickson says that as a youngster he used to break into Taronga Park Zoo, even though he was a zoo club member and could get in free.[66] People do destructive things for no apparent reason. It is the human heart which is corrupt.

Qoheleth realizes that folly has a disproportionate effect: 'Dead flies make the perfumer's ointment give off a stench; so a little folly outweighs wisdom and honour' (*Eccles.* 10:1). If I gave you a cup of tea and you found a fly in it, you would not be impressed by the argument that the cup held more tea than fly. The fact that the tea makes up 99% of the cup does not make up for the fact that the fly occupies the other 1%. In a fallen world, the downside of life seems to easily outweigh the upside. The car may be 99% right but one little thing stops it working. It will only take a small mistake for all the painstaking work of an accountant or an engineer to be rendered useless.

---

[64] Charles Bridges, *Ecclesiastes* (Edinburgh: Banner of Truth, reprinted 1981), p. 76.

[65] Richard Ingrams, *God's Apology* (Exeter: Readers Union, 1978), p. 250.

[66] John Dickson, *A Sneaking Suspicion* (Kingsford: St Matthias Press, 1993), p. 45.

You may have heard of the man in the lunatic asylum who sent a very cogent and well-argued letter to the governor saying why he should be released. All of his arguments were compelling, and he seemed to have made his case in a way that was incontrovertible. He did an excellent job until he came to sign the letter. Then his mission came to grief. He signed the letter 'Napoleon', and the governor refused his request.

A person may do fairly well but one fall has a disastrous effect on him and on those around him. What do you remember of the life of King David? Surely it is his fight with Goliath and his adultery with Bathsheba. And what about King Manasseh? Despite his conversion to God, and his attempts at the end to right his long life of wrong, he could not reverse the effects of his evil reign. Our folly will have a disproportionate effect on our lives. The fool raves on but adds nothing to the wisdom of the world, yet he cannot even find the way to town: 'A fool multiplies words, though no man knows what is to be, and who can tell him what will be after him? The toil of a fool wearies him, for he does not know the way to the city' (*Eccles.* 10:14–15).

The world is not as it ought to be. There is folly everywhere. The fool cannot walk down the road without showing that he is a fool (*Eccles.* 10:3). The world is upside down: 'There is an evil that I have seen under the sun, as it were an error proceeding from the ruler: folly is set in many high places, and the rich sit in a low place. I have seen slaves on horses, and princes on the ground like slaves' (*Eccles.* 10:5–7).

The wrong people so often end up in power. The Bible says that there are fools in high places – and human nature has not changed down through the years. Back in ancient times, the Roman emperor Caligula had his horse elected to the

Senate. To the long-suffering subjects of the Roman Empire, Caligula's horse would surely have been more welcome as a Senator than the depraved and brutal Caligula himself. In the West, elections have descended into publicity stunts and image production. Democracy has increasingly become a mirage put together by media-inspired conjuring tricks.

Read through *First and Second Kings* in the Old Testament. Are not most of the kings fools or criminals? Even the best ones can be weak at crucial times. When the wrong person is in power, the result is woe, not blessing: 'Woe to you, O land, when your king is a child, and your princes feast in the morning! Happy are you, O land, when your king is the son of the nobility, and your princes feast at the proper time, for strength, and not for drunkenness!' (*Eccles.* 10:16–17). It is as Augustine said: 'Remove justice, and what are kingdoms but gangs of criminals on a large scale?'[67]

Yet it can be dangerous to point this out – one never knows who is listening and what might happen. 'Even in your thought, do not curse the king, nor in your bedroom curse the rich, for a bird of the air will carry your voice, or some winged creature tell the matter' (*Eccles.* 10:20). A little bird can be your undoing.

Life is out of kilter: 'He who digs a pit will fall into it, and a serpent will bite him who breaks through a wall. He who quarries stones is hurt by them, and he who splits logs is endangered by them. If the iron is blunt, and one does not sharpen the edge, he must use more strength, but wisdom helps one to succeed' (*Eccles.* 10:8–10). Despite what some commentators say, this does not seem like moral retribution – sin and you get punished, do right and you get blessed. It

---

[67] Augustine, *The City of God* IV, 4.

does not work out so neatly. Wisdom is better than brute strength. But things just seem to happen. Things just go wrong. The fireman retrieves the kitten from the tree, then accidentally runs over it. The farmer digs a pit for water, but falls into it. A man breaks through a wall but is bitten by a snake. There are dangers in the everyday things of life that we do.

Ecclesiastes is a realistic book. It deals with life as it is, not life as one might wish it to be. Fanatics who refuse to face reality have done terrible harm to the world. In 1922 H. G. Wells published *A Short History of the World*. At the end of his book, Wells wrote: 'As yet we are hardly in the earliest dawn of human greatness . . . What man has done, the little triumphs of his present state, and all this history we have told, form but the prelude to the things that man has yet to do.' He asked: 'Can we doubt that presently our race will more than realize our boldest imaginations, that it will achieve unity and peace, that it will live, the children of our blood and lives will live, in a world made more splendid and lovely than any palace or garden that we know, going on from strength to strength in an ever widening circle of adventure and achievement?' It should be pointed out that science fiction, not history – and certainly not prophecy – was Wells' forte.

This quest for perfection – and belief that it was attainable – was characteristic of the late nineteenth and early twentieth centuries. In Christian circles, it led to the teaching of perfectionism, that Christians could actually become perfect in this life. It was behind a lot of the naïve political thinking of the day whereby people such as Sidney and Beatrice Webb became convinced that the Soviet tyranny of the 1930s and 1940s was actually a new civilization, worthy of all admiration and imitation. Victor Gollancz visited the USSR in 1937, and was delighted with what he saw: 'For the first time I have been completely happy . . . while here one can forget the evil in the rest of the world.'[68] Apparently he missed the show trials, the forced collectivization, the purges, the man-made famines, and the concentration camps.

In Germany the notion of utopianism could be found in the Nazi 'Master Race' theory. Those who did not measure up – Jews, gypsies, and the physically and mentally unfit – were eradicated. Hence Dietrich Bonhoeffer's lament that 'The vilest contempt for mankind goes about its sinister business with the holiest protestations of devotion to the human cause.'[69]

Another manifestation of this idea can be found in the Eugenics Societies which existed in most Western countries before World War 2.[70] The Nazis managed to give eugenics a bad name, but not dissimilar views continue to prevail today. The various Family Planning Associations (known as Planned Parenthood in the USA) began life as Eugenics Societies dedicated to the principle of racial improvement. In Australia the New South Wales Family Planning Association was, until 1960, known as the Racial Hygiene Association. Social Engineering has always been its aim.

Now we are seeing that same philosophy taken the next step. Having children is increasingly becoming a kind of

[68] Cited in Paul Johnson, *Intellectuals* (London: Weidenfeld & Nicolson, 1988), p. 280.
[69] Dietrich Bonhoeffer, *Ethics* ed. by E. Bethge (London: SCM, 1971), p. 54.
[70] See Stefan Kühl, *The Nazi Connection: Eugenics, American Racism, and German National Socialism* (New York: Oxford University Press, 2002).

shopping experience. Babies are supposed to be defect-free or their lives are forfeit. Genetic testing is being used to 'weed out' undesirables, and produce the 'perfect' baby. There are an increasing number of cases before Western courts where people with disabilities are suing their doctors and perhaps even their mothers for 'wrongful life'. In effect, they are suing because they were not aborted. The demand for perfection can produce tyranny, a cheapening of life, and degradation.

Yet Christianity too demands perfection. Christ commands us to be perfect as our Father in heaven is perfect (*Matt.* 5:48). God's ways are perfect (*Psa.* 18:30), and we are to walk in his ways. There is, however, a considerable difference between the biblical view of perfection and the various worldly views. Paul said that he strove for perfection, while realizing that he had not attained it (*Phil.* 3:12–14). Indeed, we cannot attain it in this life. It is part and parcel of the limitations of this earthly existence that here we see in a mirror, dimly, and know only in part (*1 Cor.* 13:12). Before we are outraged by the sin we see on the six o'clock news, we need to be humbled by the sin we see in the mirror.

H. G. Wells' view of life led him from idiotic optimism to dark despair. It was Wells who declared hopefully of the 1914–1918 conflict, that it was 'not merely another war, – it is the last war.' Such optimism rarely survives an encounter with reality. His last book, written in 1945, was entitled *Mind at the End of Its Tether.* Sadly, that is how he died. The Christian quest for perfection does not lead to despair; it leads to humility. For we recognize that we will never attain perfection by ourselves. In repentance, we see that our only hope is in Christ: 'For by one offering He has perfected forever those who are being sanctified' (*Heb.* 10:14).

H. G. Wells rejected any belief in the Fall, and any subsequent understanding of the limitations of humanity. The Christian, on the other hand, is conscious of the awful reality of human sin. This is what keeps people from the kind of presumptuous folly which infected Wells' thinking. But it does not make us content with sin. While recognizing its reality, the Christian rejoices that Christ has overcome it, and that in heaven it will be no more.

George Orwell was not a professing Christian, but he did come to see the dangers in the humanistic quest for heaven on earth. Orwell wrote: 'One cannot have any worthwhile picture of the future unless one realizes how much we have lost by the decay of Christianity.' With much perception, Orwell added: 'And the Catholic intellectuals who cling to the letter of the Creeds while reading into them meanings they were never meant to have, and who snigger at anyone simple enough to suppose that the Fathers of the Church meant what they said, are simply raising smoke-screens to conceal their own disbelief from themselves.'[71] Orwell was groping towards an understanding of the problem that faces all humanity – how to know right from wrong, and how to live meaningfully in a world that is a long way from being perfect. Ultimately, the quest for perfection can lead to Auschwitz or the Gulag, but it can also lead us to the foot of the cross and ultimately to heaven.

What about the will of the people? Is not what they express sacrosanct in this age of democracy? Yet there are dangers lurking just below the surface. 'Better was a poor and wise youth than an old and foolish king who no longer knew how to take advice. For he went from prison to the throne, though

---

[71] George Orwell, 'As I Please' in *Tribune* 3 March 1944.

in his own kingdom he had been born poor. I saw all the living who move about under the sun, along with that youth who was to stand in the king's place. There was no end of all the people, all of whom he led. Yet those who come later will not rejoice in him. Surely this also is vanity and a striving after wind' (*Eccles.* 4:13–16).

No one is a hero for long. Pop stars, film stars, sporting heroes, and political leaders are but for a moment. Tremper Longman III thinks that political power may be especially in view here. A government is hardly in power before many think that the best thing to do is tip it out. Caesar is murdered, and the crowd is swayed in favour of the act first by Brutus, then against it by Mark Antony. Almost anybody can sound convincing to a people with flexible principles. One day they proclaim 'Hosanna! Blessed is he who comes in the name of the Lord!' but before the week is out, the cry is 'Crucify him!'

'I have also seen the example of wisdom under the sun, and it seemed great to me. There was a little city with few men in it, and a great king came against it and besieged it, building great siege works against it. But there was found in it a poor, wise man, and he by his wisdom delivered the city. Yet no one remembered that poor man. But I say that wisdom is better than might, though the poor man's wisdom is despised and his words are not heard' (*Eccles.* 9:13–16).

This little story has been enacted in real life many times down through the ages. In Cervantes' comic masterpiece, *Don Quixote*, the hero liberates the slaves, and expects their undying gratitude, but instead they turn on him. In 1650 Oliver Cromwell was travelling through Northampton with John Lambert who was impressed by the cheering crowd. Cromwell was more realistic: 'These very persons would shout as much if you and I were going to be hanged.'[72] In more modern times, Winston Churchill led Great Britain during the terrible years of World War II, then in 1945 he was swept from office in a result which shocked and hurt him. At times nothing fails like success.

It is not just in the political arena that popularity can be short-lived and begin to pall. If you live for popularity, you will find yourself miserable at the futility of it all. After winning two successive Wimbledons, in 1985 and 1986, when only 17, then 18, years of age, Boris Becker had soared to the top of the tennis world. The next year he attempted suicide.

The film world is no more satisfying. Michael Caine said that in Hollywood, you never mixed with anyone who had failed. There is glamour and glitter galore, but little of substance or real goodness. So much of it is narcissistic. As Evelyn Waugh commented on Hollywood: 'All is a continuous psalm of self-praise.'[73]

Major-General Charles Gordon in the nineteenth century once sneered that human glory is ninety-nine per cent twaddle.[74] He probably underestimated reality. Logie awards, Academy awards, knighthoods, acclaim in the media – all mean nothing. The child with Down's Syndrome who smiles at his parents, the ditch-digger who labours to support his family, the wife who faithfully carries on in difficult circumstances – these all contribute far more to the sum total of human happiness and goodness.

---

[72] Christopher Hill, *God's Englishman* (Harmondsworth: Penguin, 1979), pp. 188–189.

[73] Cited in K. L. Billingsley, *The Seductive Image: A Christian Critique of the World of Film* (Illinois: Crossway, 1989), p. 111.

[74] Mark Bryant, *Private Lives*, (London: Cassell & Co, 2001), p. 172.

Utopians – unrealistic people who have tried to establish a perfect society on earth – have done an enormous amount of harm throughout history. We are to entertain no delusions of adequacy. Simone Weil once commented that 'The root of evil . . . is daydreaming.'[75] That sounds an odd way to put it, but it is correct. People dream wrong things before they do wrong things. Is that not the way it works? Every sin we ever commit has its beginning in our thoughts. When we have capitulated in our thoughts we have sinned.

There is a need to be realistic about what good can be achieved in a fallen world. To cite Bonhoeffer: 'The liberation of man as an absolute ideal leads only to man's self-destruction.'[76] Hugh Kingsmill is equally perceptive: 'Utopianism is the transference to society of the individual's disappointed expectation of personal happiness.'[77] This is a recipe for tragedy and tyranny. All human achievements undermine themselves. Fierce radicalism hates compromise, but ends up with tyranny; compromise hates ideals, but ends up with mediocrity.

Democracy without a basis in righteousness can descend into demagoguery, debauchery and dictatorship. In fact, Western democracies are becoming increasingly chaotic and coercive at the same time. Freedom and order are losing their Christian meanings. To survive, democracy requires two things: moral goodness and moral realism. Those two things are not found in vast quantities in the Western world at the moment.

[75] Simone Pétrement, *Simone Weil*, trans. by Raymond Rosenthal (London: Mowbrays, 1976), p. 465.

[76] Dietrich Bonhoeffer, *Ethics* p. 82.

[77] Hugh Kingsmill, *The Poisoned Crown* p. 7.

One of Australia's most popular Prime Ministers was Bob Hawke. He once made the promise that by the year 1991 no Australian child would be living in poverty. What he actually achieved was that no Australian ex-Prime Minister would be living in poverty. Dr Johnson had a Christian scepticism about the dreams postulated by political thinkers and the promises uttered by political candidates. He told Boswell that 'most schemes of political improvement are very laughable things'.[78]

William Blake touched on the perpetual problem of fallen humanity in dealing with politics:

> *The iron hand crushed the Tyrant's head*
> *And became a tyrant in his stead.*

Not for nothing did Dietrich Bonhoeffer remind us that the first message of the church to the state was not 'Make politics Christian' but 'recognize finitude'.[79] That might have been phrased more simply, but Bonhoeffer was recognizing two things: the universal sinfulness of all humanity, and God's refusal to grant all-embracing power to any one human being or institution, even the church. Knowing our limitations is part of the fear of the Lord which is the beginning of wisdom.

It was the 'Iron Chancellor', Otto von Bismarck, who suggested that the making of laws was rather like the making of sausages – it was best if one did not actually see how it was done. Those who fail to recognize human limitations but who insist on creating paradise on earth only end up creating

[78] James Boswell, *The Life of Samuel Johnson Vol. 1* (London: Dent, reprinted 1973), p. 374.

[79] Dietrich Bonhoeffer, *No Rusty Swords* (London: Fontana, 1970), p. 152.

tyranny on earth. It is not at all uncommon for politicians and activists to work themselves up into a lather of moral indignation over a social issue while their private lives are neatly cordoned off from all criticism – especially self-criticism.

Robert Conquest has put forward the thesis that the main responsibility for the moral disasters of the twentieth century lies not so much in the problems as in the solutions. The solutions have all looked plausible, but have proved to be defective and delusive. The result has been savagery at the hands of rogue ideologies.[80]

Whether it be Plato's dream of rule by philosopher-kings, Rousseau's extolling of the noble savage who is uncorrupted by civilization, Karl Marx's vision of the dictatorship of the proletariat leading to the withering away of the state, Margaret Mead's delusions about the happy Samoans free of all sexual taboos, or Adolf Hitler's Thousand-Year Reich with all Aryans and no Jews, the result has always been the same – falsehood, coercion, tyranny, and corruption. Instead of the Workers' State, it is the Gulag; instead of the Thousand-Year Reich, it is Auschwitz. Seeking designer babies and the eradication of imperfection and suffering, we end up debasing human life and producing a race akin to Jonathan Swift's Yahoos. Looking for Utopia, we fall into the Inferno.

[80] See Robert Conquest, *Reflections on a Ravaged Century* (London: John Murray, 1999).

# 7

# A Touch of Religion

If all else seems to be failing, why not try religion? As you grow older, you notice that wealth has its limitations – 'You can't take it with you,' is the cliché. Also, those who profess to be wise seem to lack something when it comes to living life each day. If there is a God, a touch of religion could come in handy.

In our modern and post-modern world, tolerance has replaced love, and anti-discrimination has replaced truth. There is plenty of moralism but less morality. The Preacher is more aware of the God who, in Francis Schaeffer's words, 'is there and is not silent'. Accordingly, we need to fear him. 'Spirituality' has re-entered the vocabulary of the age, but bowing before the revealed will of the only true God is still a foreign concept to most people.

According to Dwight D. Eisenhower in the 1950s, American government made no sense 'unless it is founded in a deeply felt religious faith – and I don't care what it is'.[81] In a sense, that is true – any kind of cement may keep a building together. However, religion is not designed simply to keep

---

[81] Cited in Herbert Schlossberg, *Idols for Destruction* (Nashville: Thomas Nelson, 1983), p. 251.

society together. It is meant to tell of God, so that we can know him in a saving way. Qoheleth realized that God is not to be toyed with. He is not the means to an end, but is the goal itself.

As we have seen, Ecclesiastes tells us that we have eternity in our hearts (3:11). It also tells us that we shall all die, and our spirits shall return to God for judgment (12:7). This is not good news to everybody because God shall judge everything we have done, said and thought (12:14). This truth is the foundation for all right dealing with God.

Thomas Chalmers was a minister in the Church of Scotland, but when he first entered the ministry, he did not know the reality of God and eternity. He became well-known – or notorious – for a comment he made in 1805, that 'after the satisfactory discharge of his parish duties, a minister may enjoy five days in the week of uninterrupted leisure, for the prosecution of any science in which his taste may dispose him to engage'.[82] However, such an approach was no help to him when his brother and two of his sisters died of what was then called consumption (tuberculosis). Chalmers himself had been bed-ridden with consumption, and he took to reading Blaise Pascal's *Pensées*, and then William Wilberforce's *A Practical View*. He had also been through a broken engagement.

By 1811 he was a new man, but his former words came back to haunt him. In 1825 an opponent cited Chalmers' own words of 1805, and Chalmers had to confess his former ignorance and pride. He had to repudiate his own past views: 'I had forgotten two magnitudes – I thought not of the

---

[82] Stewart J. Brown, *Thomas Chalmers and the Godly Commonwealth in Scotland* (Oxford: Oxford University Press, 1982), p. 26.

littleness of time – I recklessly thought not of the greatness of eternity!'[83]

You can only be interested in a little bit of religion if you are concerned for a little bit of salvation. The God who created you and all the universe, and who shall judge all humanity, is not to be trifled with. Either he is everything or he is nothing. If he is not first in your priorities, he will not be second. He is either your redeemer or your judge. We dare not fool with God.

'Guard your steps when you go to the house of God. To draw near to listen is better than to offer the sacrifice of fools, for they do not know that they are doing evil. Be not rash with your mouth, nor let your heart be hasty to utter a word before God, for God is in heaven and you are on earth. Therefore let your words be few. For a dream comes with much business, and a fool's voice with many words. When you vow a vow to God, do not delay paying it, for he has no pleasure in fools. Pay what you vow. It is better that you should not vow than that you should vow and not pay. Let not your mouth lead you into sin, and do not say before the messenger that it was a mistake. Why should God be angry at your voice and destroy the work of your hands? For when dreams increase and words grow many, there is vanity; but God is the one you must fear' (*Eccles.* 5:1–7).

Derek Tidball tells of a man who was asked to say grace in Latin at Cambridge University. The poor man knew neither prayers nor Latin, but he knew something about detergents, so he intoned: 'Omo, Lux, Domestos, Brobat, Ajax, Amen.' Everybody else said 'Amen', and the meal proceeded.[84]

---

[83] S. Brown, *Thomas Chalmers* p. 181.

[84] Derek Tidball, *That's Just the Way It Is* (Fearn: Christian Focus, 1998), p. 76.

Worship can be as meaningless as that. People can be keen to make baptismal or membership vows but careless about keeping them. Ministers take vows to uphold the Thirty-Nine Articles or the Westminster Confession, but they do not believe them. People walk to the front at crusades or concerts, and yet are not converted. So much supposed faith is in fact perjury. Far better not to do anything in the first place.

Francis Schaeffer once speculated how much religious activity would still go on were the Holy Spirit to be withdrawn. His answer was that there would still be synods, services, theological research, lectures at seminaries, crusades, and the like. It is very possible to have considerable religious activity without the blessing or power of God resting upon any of it.

George Bernard Shaw came to extol the Life Force, and crusaded against the eating of meat. Recently we have seen the explosion of such thinking in the New Age movement. All very noble in a way, but ultimately such a view of life is neither particularly comforting nor particularly challenging. C. S. Lewis referred to it as 'a sort of tame God. You can switch it on when you want, but it will not bother you. All the thrills of religion and none of the cost.'[85]

In 1986, the doyen of Australian historians, Professor Manning Clark, stated that this generation is probably the first one in our history to believe in absolutely nothing. Previous generations for the most part believed in Christianity or the echo of Christianity. But now they often have not got the faintest idea of what it is about.[86] Not long ago, a woman and the man she was living with came into my

---

[85] C. S. Lewis, *Mere Christianity*, 1975 reprint, p. 34.

[86] Cited in B. A. Santamaria, *Australia at the Crossroads* (Melbourne University Press, 1987), p. 150.

study to inquire about a wedding. We had hardly started the interview, when she delivered a remarkable sermon about how she wanted to follow the Christian teaching on the permanency of marriage. Indeed, that was why she had been living with her partner for the last four years – to see whether she could live with him permanently. She honestly believed that was the Christian way. For quite a few moments, I could do nothing but look blank.

Sin means that we dare not treat God lightly. God is true but we are not. We all profess to hate hypocrisy and to love authenticity. John Bunyan was deeply impressed that the women of Bedford could talk earnestly about God and salvation, and mean every word of it. Yet such is our perversity that people are often eager to take religious vows that they do not really believe.

God is the God of truth. Carl Jung declared that 'Religion helps one to live . . . I care not about the existence debate.'[87] But better to face the truth rather than live a delusion. The apostle Paul said that if Christ did not rise from the dead, then Christians were the most pitiable people on earth (*1 Cor.* 15:19). Believing in God or in Christ's resurrection will only help you if God actually exists and if Christ has risen, never to die again. You might believe in a religion because it works. It is far better to believe in a religion because it is true. There are people who believe that flying saucers will transport them to paradise or that certain herbs will enable them to live forever in good health. But defying the law of gravity does not mean that you can step off tall buildings without disastrous consequences.

[87] Cited in Dick Gross, *Godless Gospel* (Annandale: Pluto Press, 1999), p. 33.

It has been said that false hope is better than no hope at all. On this ground, an attorney in Atlanta in 1995 refused to tell a condemned criminal that his last appeal had failed, and that his execution was very imminent.[88] Falsehood makes the world go round. God tells us that there is hope for all who are earnest about the truth. To lie on oath in a court of law is perjury, and taken very seriously. How much worse is it to take a vow before God, and not mean it.

Nevertheless, there is hope for all who love truth. As Simone Weil expressed it, in words that one can only hope are true: 'Christ likes us to prefer truth to him because, before being Christ, he is truth. If one turns aside from him to go to the truth, one will not go far before falling into his arms.'[89]

[88] Cited in Dick Gross, *Godless Gospel* p. 144.
[89] Simone Weil, *Waiting on God* (London: Fontana, reprinted 1973), p. 36.

# 8

# The Consolations of Life

There are dangers in doing what we have been doing. We have arrived at the point where we have seen that there is something wrong with everything. Goethe said that it is much easier to recognize error than to find truth.[90] It is necessary for the truth's sake that we recognize falsehood wherever we find it, and know that falsehood abounds in this world. Nevertheless, left by itself, this truth may harm us. It may lead us into unpleasant habits of criticizing everything. Given the state of the world, and the human condition, it is, as Juvenal said, 'hard not to write satire'.[91]

Because of this danger, A. W. Tozer warned about the possibility of earnest Christians falling into the sour habit of fault-finding. He wrote: 'What makes this cynical spirit particularly dangerous is that the cynic is usually right. His analyses are accurate, his judgment sound; yet for all that he is wrong, frightfully, pathetically wrong.' As a cure, Tozer recommended the cultivation of a spirit of thankfulness.[92]

[90] Cited in Jeremy Campbell, *The Liar's Tale: A History of Falsehood* (New York: W. W. Norton & Co, 2001), p. 43.
[91] Cited in Terry Lindvall, *Surprised by Laughter* (Nashville: Thomas Nelson, 1996), p. 327.
[92] A. W. Tozer, *Gems from Tozer* (Kent: STL Books, 1978), p. 66.

A thankful heart should be discerning, but it cannot be cynical.

The message of Ecclesiastes is not that this world is so awful that we ought to look to a better one. There is some truth in that outlook, but it is also true that there are very real consolations in this life. Ecclesiastes is an earthy book. Indeed, the Bible itself is both heavenly and earthy in its approach to life. It is certainly not naïve, nor is it fanatical.

Qoheleth mentions friendship as one of the consolations of life. Toiling by oneself for oneself is vanity and an unhappy business (*Eccles.* 4:7–8), but the story does not end there. 'Two are better than one, because they have a good reward for their toil. For if they fall, one will lift up his fellow. But woe to him who is alone when he falls and has not another to lift him up! Again, if two lie together, they keep warm, but how can one keep warm alone? And though a man might prevail against one who is alone, two will withstand him – a threefold cord is not quickly broken' (*Eccles.* 4:9–12).

Friendship is one of the few real and substantial consolations that we have in this world. Jean-Paul Sartre's view was that 'hell is other people', but most people will see through that, and will say that they value friendship. When Horace lost his friend, he thought that he had lost half his soul. Loneliness is one of the greatest afflictions in this world. It is surely instructive that Jesus sent out his disciples two by two (see *Luke* 10).

Interestingly enough, this passage from the fourth chapter of Ecclesiastes was actually the text of George Whitefield's first sermon. At the funeral of George Whitefield in 1771, John Wesley said that Whitefield's capacity for friendship was 'the distinguishing part of his character'.[93] Friends are a help in trouble (*Eccles.* 4:10), in danger (*Eccles.* 4:12), and in the cold (*Eccles.* 4:11). Verse 11 is referring to travelling at night. A lone traveller would lie close to his donkey for warmth. So friendship that is genuine means that life is not totally futile here on earth.

It is true that friendship, like everything else in a world like this, can be corrupted. We are warned that 'Bad company ruins good morals' (*1 Cor.* 15:33). Many a man has done in bad company what he would not do alone. As a youth, Augustine, along with some friends, stole some pears and threw them at pigs. Later, he commented that 'our real pleasure consisted in doing something that was forbidden'.[94] Such is the perversity of the human heart that it simply loves sinning. Yet Augustine was sure that he would never have done this alone. Peer pressure is a powerful influence, and it can push us one way or the other. If friends can be a help to us, it is also true that they can lead us astray.

For all that, we are meant to perceive life as God's good gift to us: 'Behold, what I have seen to be good and fitting is to eat and drink and find enjoyment in all the toil with which one toils under the sun the few days of his life that God has given him, for this is his lot. Everyone also to whom God has given wealth and possessions and power to enjoy them, and to accept his lot and rejoice in his toil – this is the gift of God. For he will not much remember the days of his life because God keeps him occupied with joy in his heart' (*Eccles.* 5:18–20).

---

[93] A. Dallimore, *George Whitefield, Vol. 2* (Edinburgh: Banner of Truth, 1980), p. 511.

[94] Augustine, *Confessions* II, 4.

Work and wealth are futile apart from God. Where do they lead? Does work keep me from sin and death? No, and neither does wealth. But if I see them as God's gift, then I have a totally different perspective. This is the key to it all. Voltaire, in *Candide*, looked at all the things that are wrong with the world, and argued that therefore there is no God ruling it. Dr Samuel Johnson, in *Rasselas*, looked at the same fallen world, and said this showed that there was a God who would right all wrongs.

It is perspective that is crucial. How will you wake up tomorrow morning? Will you ask: 'What is the point in this rat race?' Or will you say: 'This is the day that the LORD has made; I will rejoice and be glad in it' (*Psa.* 118:24)? In the ordinary things of life – in work, in money, in friendship, even in the things that are wrong – the Christian sees a God-given purpose. What is your perspective on life?

The consolations we have in this life are real, but limited. We can eat, drink, and be merry: 'And I commend joy, for man has no good thing under the sun but to eat and drink and be joyful, for this will go with him in his toil through the days of his life that God has given him under the sun' (*Eccles.* 8:15). The Bible advocates self-control, but it is not ascetic in a Hindu sense. It sees no virtue in lying on a bed of nails for three days. 'Go, eat your bread in joy, and drink your wine with a merry heart, for God has already approved what you do. Let your garments be always white. Let not oil be lacking on your head' (*Eccles.* 9:7–8). Pleasure is an empty and onerous god, but a delightful and needed companion.

Monasticism is, in essence, a false move. When it emerged within Christianity in the fourth century, men would refuse to meet with women, even their mothers and sisters; they would not bathe for months; they ate as little as possible; and they tried to go without sleep – or, failing that, they would try to sleep while standing up. 'Enjoy life with the wife whom you love, all the days of your vain life that he has given you under the sun, because that is your portion in life and in your toil at which you toil under the sun' (*Eccles. 9:9*).

We are meant to work on with conviction: 'Whatever your hand finds to do, do it with your might, for there is no work or thought or knowledge or wisdom in Sheol, to which you are going' (*Eccles. 9:10*). Work becomes idolatrous when we live for it, but we are better off working than not working. As Adam puts it in Milton's *Paradise Lost*: 'With labour I must earn my bread; what harm? Idleness had been worse'.[95]

Oliver Wendell Holmes took up the study of Greek at the age of ninety-four and when asked why, replied: 'It's now or never.' True enough, I suppose, but at that age there are other things to think about. If death ends everything, what do we have left? We are to be joyful, enjoy our families, and work well – but so what if it all ends in death? John Maynard Keynes pointed out that in the long run we are all dead. That is the great fact which we must all deal with. Our view of death will determine our view of life.

The only way to cope with life is to work on, despite all its uncertainties. 'Cast your bread upon the waters, for you will find it after many days. Give a portion to seven, or even to eight, for you know not what disaster may happen on earth. If the clouds are full of rain, they empty themselves on the earth, and if a tree falls to the south or to the north, in the place where the tree falls, there it will lie. He who observes the wind will not sow, and he who regards the clouds will not reap. As you do not know the way the spirit comes to the

---

[95] John Milton, *Paradise Lost*, X, 1054–1055.

bones in the womb of a woman with child, so you do not know the work of God who makes everything. In the morning sow your seed, and at evening withhold not your hand, for you do not know which will prosper, this or that, or whether both alike will be good' (*Eccles.* 11:1–6).

In some circles this is often quoted in favour of giving to charity – the idea being, give because you never know whether it will come back to you. But it is also to do with business and work. Because life is uncertain, diversify your work and investments. In fact, it is applicable to all areas of life. Work while it is still day (*John* 9:4).

We do not know everything – we do not know the way of the wind or how the unborn baby grows in his mother's womb nor do we know what God will do (*Eccles.* 11:5). We do not control the rainfall or the fall of a tree (*Eccles.* 11:3), but the right response to that is not: 'I do not know if this will work so I won't do anything. It might rain so we won't go on the picnic or I won't wash the car or put out the washing.' If you are always trying to foresee problems, you will see plenty, and you will do nothing. That is not the way to live life. It is the sluggard who says, 'There is a lion outside! I shall be killed in the streets!' (*Prov.* 22:13).

Sometimes the problem is not so much laziness as a deadening despondency. It may be that a person just gives up on life. 'No,' says the Scripture, 'Get down to work, and do what you have to do. Plant your crops, fix your plumbing, make that piece of furniture, hand out that tract, teach that class – there will always be reasons not to get out of bed in the morning. Some of your most significant acts will be those you did not think twice about.' The fact that we do not know if a project will be successful or not is not the point. It is not for us to know the results; it is for us to do our duty.

The pessimist is in danger of being paralysed; the optimist is in danger of being unrealistic. The Bible is realistic but tells us to press on regardless. As Woody Allen pessimistically saw it: 'More than at any time in history, mankind stands at a crossroad. One path leads to despair and utter hopelessness; the other leads to total extinction. Let us pray that we have the wisdom to choose correctly!'[96] Without faith, that is probably a reasonable position. Folly does have a disproportionate effect, this life is out of kilter, we are ruled by idiots, and there is every reason to despair as Woody Allen does. But God says: 'Cast your bread upon the waters. Some things may fail, but by God's grace some will succeed.' For the Christian, this means we have every incentive to preach the Word in season and out of season (*2 Tim.* 4:2), for God's Word shall not return unto him empty or void (*Isa.* 55:10).

The believer in Christ walks by faith, not by sight, but he is still to walk, to do his duty, and to persevere in what is right and good. Life has purpose under God. It is not a case of one pointless thing after another. Every detail has its part to play in the overall purpose. 'For everything there is a season, and a time for every matter under heaven: a time to be born, and a time to die; a time to plant, and a time to pluck up what is planted; a time to kill, and a time to heal; a time to break down, and a time to build up; a time to weep, and a time to laugh; a time to mourn, and a time to dance; a time to cast away stones, and a time to gather stones together; a time to embrace, and a time to refrain from embracing; a time to seek, and a time to lose; a time to keep, and a time to cast away; a time to tear, and a time to sew; a time to keep silence,

---

[96] Cited in M. Green and G. Carkner, *Ten Myths About Christianity* (Lion, 1988), p. 18.

and a time to speak; a time to love, and a time to hate; a time for war, and a time for peace' (*Eccles.* 3:1–8).

What gives life meaning? The Preacher struggles, but answers: 'I perceived that whatever God does endures forever; nothing can be added to it, nor anything taken from it. God has done it, so that people fear before him' (*Eccles.* 3:14). Life derives its meaning from God. His work is forever; he will judge all things. God alone is the source of life, and the victor over death. He will raise each one of us, and judge us.

If there is no resurrection, 'Let us eat and drink, for tomorrow we die' (*1 Cor.* 15:32). But if there is a resurrection, we have every reason to be 'steadfast, immovable, always abounding in the work of the Lord, knowing that in the Lord your labour is not in vain' (*1 Cor.* 15:58). Jonathan Edwards wrote in his diary: 'Resolved never to do anything, which I should be afraid to do if it were the last hour of my life.'[97] Joseph Hall wrote in a similar vein: 'Each day is a new life, and an abridgment of the whole. I will so live, as if I counted every day my first and my last; as if I began to live but then, and should live no more afterwards.'[98] Death followed by judgment means that everything is meaningful. Death followed by rotting in the grave means that nothing is meaningful.

Two people may be doing similar things, yet not the same thing. Two students may be studying at university. One comes to the conclusion that it is all pointless, and takes to drugs to relieve the boredom. The other labours for the glory of God.

---

[97] Jonathan Edwards, *Works, Vol. 1* (Edinburgh: Banner of Truth, reprinted 1976), p. xx.

[98] Joseph Hall, *Contemplations*, p. xviii.

Two men are at a party. One is frantic to extract every ounce of pleasure that he can out of it – he drinks, he clowns about, he chases any woman who looks sideways at him. The other man enjoys himself but pleasure is not his god. Two mothers are wiping runny noses and cleaning dishes. One sees this as meaningless drudgery; the other sees it as preparing another generation for eternity.

Wisdom, pleasure, and work cannot stand on their own two feet. They require a foundation, and that foundation is the God of eternity. There are real consolations in this life, for believer and unbeliever alike. There are children, there are the beauties and intricacies of nature, there is poetry and music, and the joy of human relationships. But these require a perspective, which comes from outside this world. As Augustine of Hippo so beautifully put it: 'God, then, had given you all these things. Love Him who made them.'[99]

---

[99] P. Brown, *Augustine of Hippo* (London: Faber and Faber, 2000), p. 325

# 9

# Know What You Don't Know

John Calvin commented that 'To be ignorant of things which it is neither possible nor lawful to know is to be learned.'[100] He preached: 'For it is the greatest wisdom that can be in men, not to be inquisitive of further things than God has revealed unto them, and simply to content themselves with that which they are able to conceive.'[101] Trying to know more than what is possible for us to know is not to pursue wisdom but folly.

On the one hand, life is very predictable – the same thing day in and day out. Life is an endless round of catching trains, driving cars, eating meals, watching television, paying bills, filling in forms, pulling out weeds, trying to keep ahead of an avalanche of problems. Vanity, vanity, all is vanity – and very predictable vanity at that. Yet, on the other hand, there are many uncertainties in life. In order that our limitations do us least harm, we need to know what they are.

The wise person knows that, as a fallen human being, he or she is very limited. There is always far more that we do not

[100] W. J. Bouwsma, *John Calvin* (Oxford: Oxford University Press, 1988), p. 155 (although Bouwsma gives the wrong reference).
[101] John Calvin, *Sermons on Deuteronomy* (Edinburgh: Banner of Truth, facsimile edition 1987), p. 1044 (slightly modernized).

know than what we do know. For example, we do not know the future. 'Whatever has come to be has already been named, and it is known what man is, and that he is not able to dispute with one stronger than he. The more words, the more vanity, and what is the advantage to man? For who knows what is good for man while he lives the few days of his vain life, which he passes like a shadow? For who can tell man what will be after him under the sun?' (*Eccles*. 6:10–12). Indeed, 'he does not know what is to be, for who can tell him how it will be?' (*Eccles*. 8:7).

Wisdom is good so far as it goes, but who can tell you what the future will bring? God can, but he is not telling – not in localized detail anyway. We plot and plan, but should remember that we always need to say: 'If the Lord wills, we will live and do this or that' (see *James* 4:13–16). We can pretend that these things are not true. Eugene Christian once wrote a book entitled *How to Live to Be a Hundred*. Alas, he died at 69.

I cannot tell you what will happen tomorrow. Neither can the astrologer. Life is wrapped with uncertainties. Christianity gives us the big picture – Christ will come again and judge the whole earth, gathering his people to himself, and punishing his enemies with everlasting judgment. That is the big picture, but the small picture of what is going to happen tomorrow is beyond you and me. There may be a wonderful opportunity, there may be terrible tragedy, or there may be just another day.

Another thing which often leaves us baffled is the work-ings of life: 'In my vain life I have seen everything. There is a righteous man who perishes in his righteousness, and there is a wicked man who prolongs his life in his evildoing' (*Eccles*. 7:15). Or, as Qoheleth puts it later, 'There is a vanity that takes place on earth, that there are righteous people to whom it happens according to the deeds of the wicked, and there are wicked people to whom it happens according to the deeds of the righteous. I said that this is also vanity' (*Eccles.* 8:14).

It seems unfair. A person may get killed while helping someone else, while another lives on in his wicked ways. The godly Scottish minister, Robert Murray M'Cheyne died before he was thirty, while the fierce sceptic, Bertrand Russell, made it to 98. In October 1889 the Headmaster of Caulfield Grammar School in Melbourne, Joseph Henry Davies, was ordained in the Presbyterian Church of Victoria, and left to become a missionary in Korea. Within a few months he was dead, at the age of 33, as a result of smallpox complicated by pneumonia. Yet Josef Stalin was allowed to tyrannize Russia for almost three decades, until his death in 1953.

Providence is a mysterious thing. Why some things happen, and others do not, is beyond us. Wisdom is something to aspire to, but we cannot quite achieve it: 'All this I have tested by wisdom. I said, "I will be wise," but it was far from me. That which has been is far off, and deep, very deep; who can find it out?' (*Eccles.* 7:23–24). The universe can seem not to be ordered at all, but subject to the random events of time and chance: 'Again I saw that under the sun the race is not to the swift, nor the battle to the strong, nor bread to the wise, nor riches to the intelligent, nor favour to those with knowledge, but time and chance happen to them all. For man does not know his time. Like fish that are taken in an evil net, and like birds that are caught in a snare, so the children of man are snared in an evil time, when it suddenly falls upon them' (*Eccles.* 9:11–12).

Success is always uncertain. The favourite does not always win, in sport, in war, in the commercial world. A 'sure thing' is beaten. The athlete falls over, the stronger army loses its way, the brilliant scholar misunderstands a crucial point. One person is acclaimed for no particular reason while another is rejected, despite being his apparent equal. One singer goes to the top of the charts, another remains unknown. It is not easy to explain why. Life can be unpredictable, and disaster may not be far away.

Australians are renowned for being obsessive about their sport, but not in the arena of ice skating. Yet in the Winter Olympics of 2002, Australia won its first ever winter Olympic gold medal when a 28-year-old from Brisbane, Steve Bradbury, managed to win his race after his four competitors fell over within fifteen metres of the finishing line. Bradbury, who had only survived the quarter-final and semi-final because of falls and a disqualification, breezed past his rivals, and went from last to first place. The swift do not always win the race. As a bemused Bradbury himself put it: 'God smiles on you some days and this is my day.'[102]

On 11 September 2001 thousands died when two planes hijacked by terrorists slammed into the Twin Towers in New York. But some people survived for extraordinary reasons – one man was late getting to work that day because his son started kindergarten; another had left the building because it was his turn to buy the doughnuts; yet another was wearing new shoes that had caused a blister to appear on his foot, so he stopped to buy a band-aid.[103] The cliché is: 'Take control of your life.' The truth is that so much of our lives is outside our control.

We can never fully understand how the world works. We are limited in ourselves. George Santayana is often quoted:

---

[102] *Sydney Morning Herald*, 18 February 2002.
[103] Source unknown – recorded on an e-mail I received.

'Those who cannot remember the past are condemned to repeat it.' The truth is more terrible than that. Even those who try to learn from the past have a habit of learning the wrong lessons. The arms race supposedly caused World War 1; appeasement supposedly caused World War 2. What, then, should determine our policy on military spending? Do arms races cause wars or do policies of appeasement? Or do both lead to war?

The trouble is that to our finite minds, just about anything can sound plausible. It is as Blaise Pascal said: 'The last stage of reason is to recognize that there is an infinity of things which surpass it. Reason is but feeble if it does not go so far as to know that.'[104] Near the end of his life, Pascal's fellow-scientist, Isaac Newton, wrote: 'I do not know how I may appear to the world; but to myself I seem to have been only like a boy, playing on the seashore, and diverting myself, in now and then finding another pebble or prettier shell than ordinary, while the great ocean of truth lay all undiscovered before me.'[105] On this earth, we are like frogs at the bottom of the well – as the Chinese proverb says, we only see part of the sky. The contemplation of what we do not know should fill us with wonder and with humility.

It is the ravages of sin which mar life in this world. 'Surely there is not a righteous man on earth who does good and never sins' (*Eccles.* 7:20). It was not ever thus: 'See, this alone I found, that God made man upright, but they have sought out many schemes' (*Eccles.* 7:29). God made us but we un-made ourselves. Wisdom is a good thing, but its consequences

---

[104] Blaise Pascal, *Pensées* p. 85.
[105] Cited in R. Hooykaas, *Religion and the Rise of Modern Science* (Michigan: Eerdmans, 1974), p. 50.

are easily undone: 'Wisdom is better than weapons of war, but one sinner destroys much good' (*Eccles.* 9:18). This is the Christian doctrine of the Fall, and of Original Sin. To cite Blaise Pascal again: 'Without this incomprehensible mystery, we are ourselves incomprehensible to our own mind.'[106]

The wisest and most righteous man still sins. All heroes have feet of clay. And so do those who debunk heroes. Sin is everywhere in this fallen world. No one escapes it. Surely we are all aware of sin, both inside and outside of us, but we do not know how to eradicate it. We know the experience of sin, but in ourselves have no solution to it.

Similarly, we know that we will die, but there are mysteries associated with life and death. 'If a man fathers a hundred children and lives many years, so that the days of his years are many, but his soul is not satisfied with life's good things, and he also has no burial, I say that a stillborn child is better off than he. For it comes in vanity and goes in darkness, and in darkness its name is covered. Moreover, it has not seen the sun or known anything, yet it finds rest rather than he. Even though he should live a thousand years twice over, yet enjoy no good – do not all go to the one place?' (*Eccles.* 6:3–6). Death is the ultimate proof of our lack of control over life: 'No man has power to retain the spirit, or power over the day of death' (*Eccles.* 8:8).

The richest man and the wisest man will die – at thirty, at fifty, at seventy, at one hundred. Who knows? The wisest thing to do is to face this: 'So teach us to number our days that we may get a heart of wisdom' (*Psa.* 90:12). The heart of wisdom tells us that our days are numbered. The beginning of wisdom is to know that we are mortal; we will die. Those who

---

[106] See Blaise Pascal, *Pensées* p. 246.

refuse to face this run aground. Marian Evans (the real name of the novelist George Eliot) found the Christian faith inconceivable, and – a true Victorian in many ways – wrote in defence of unbelief and in favour of duty. She lived with George Henry Lewes until he died in 1878. She was so grief-stricken at his death that she could not bring herself to attend his funeral. Alas, unbelief and non-attendance cannot change the harsh facts of life and death.

When life is stripped of its balloons and streamers, what matters is not learning, pleasure or wealth but goodness, that which reflects the character of God. Without that viewpoint, life becomes meaningless. You are left only with pleasure, and even that becomes pointless. People pursue pleasure but end up bored. That, more than anything else, explains the frenzy of the entertainment industry, the AIDS crisis, the drug problem, the mania for any sort of artificial excitement, and the sheer listlessness that we see in society today.

Where have we got to? Wisdom tells us that life is un-certain, and often appears unfair. It is ravaged by sin, and wisdom itself cannot not eradicate death. Wisdom also tells us that we need more than human wisdom.

Albert Camus, the novelist and existentialist, believed in Marxism, then had qualms, and came to write in *The Myth of Sisyphus*: 'There is but one philosophic problem, and that is suicide. The task of man is to respond to life's apparent meaninglessness, despair, and its absurd quality.' In other words, without God, life is meaningless, so why not suicide? But Camus, in the end, calls upon us all to fight the plague, one victim at a time, in a noble and heroic battle against the inevitable. But why is that 'better' than simply eating, drinking and being merry until we die? Camus was not so ready with an answer to that question. The only answer is that we have a God-given law within us that tells us that it is better to strive and serve than to indulge in selfish pleasures.

So now at least we know our limitations! Where does that get us? Are you any better off for knowing what you do not know? Joseph Hall prayed that God would teach him 'a sober knowledge and a contented ignorance'.[107] There is wisdom in knowing there are things we do not know and cannot know (*Deut.* 29:29). That may not be abundantly satisfying, but it is helpful. Michael Eaton says that Qoheleth is 'slamming every door except the door of faith'.[108]

[107] Joseph Hall, *Contemplations* p. 7.
[108] Michael Eaton, *Ecclesiastes* p. 108.

# 10

# Death the Giant Killjoy

It seems that in all this meandering through life, we have been led to see clearly what our problem is. In short, it is that we will all die. The Preacher drives home his hard-hitting message: you and I must face this appalling fact of death.

'It is the same for all, since the same event happens to the righteous and the wicked, to the good and the evil, to the clean and the unclean, to him who sacrifices and him who does not sacrifice. As is the good, so is the sinner, and he who swears is as he who shuns an oath. This is an evil in all that is done under the sun, that the same event happens to all. Also, the hearts of the children of man are full of evil, and madness is in their hearts while they live, and after that they go to the dead. But he who is joined with all the living has hope, for a living dog is better than a dead lion. For the living know that they will die, but the dead know nothing, and they have no more reward, for the memory of them is forgotten. Their love and their hate and their envy have already perished, and forever they have no more share in all that is done under the sun' (*Eccles.* 9:2–6).

We might read these words as the most depressing section in a depressing book. They are meant to confront us with what is obviously true. Life is tough, and then we die. Our failures are many, our victories few and meaningless, and to cap it all we look through the glass darkly. We know so little. And by the end of this chapter we may only be more certain of what we do not know.

H. T. Buckle, the nineteenth-century historian, declared that 'If immortality be untrue, it matters little whether anything else be true or not.'[109] Death hangs over everybody – over the righteous and the wicked, over the one who prays and the one who does not, over the multi-millionaire and the beggar in the gutter, over Mother Teresa and Princess Diana, over the sports star and the quadriplegic, over the one who seeks forgiveness and the one who could not care less. It can strike at any time. Eric Clapton's three-year-old son fell to his death from a New York skyscraper, leading the musician to pen his poignant song *Tears in Heaven*.

The other day the media carried a report that some doctors were researching a medical condition in the hope of reducing the mortality rate. That was not well-phrased. The mortality rate is 100%, and has always been 100% – in war and in peace, in famine and prosperity, in plague and good health, in the ancient world, the medieval world, and the modern world.

Blaise Pascal wrote bluntly: 'Imagine a number of men in chains, all under sentence of death, some of whom are each day butchered in the sight of the others; those remaining see their own condition in that of their fellows, and looking at each other with grief and despair await their turn. This is an image of the human condition.'[110] To give a fuller picture of

---

[109] Cited in T. V. Morris, *Making Sense of It All: Pascal and the Meaning of Life* (Michigan: Eerdmans, 1992), p. 26.

[110] Blaise Pascal, *Pensées* p. 165.

our life here on earth, we would want to say more than that – and Ecclesiastes does say more – but we cannot say less. Something like 95 million people die every year. Three die every second. In the time it has taken you to read this paragraph, perhaps 120 people have entered eternity. We do not cope with this fact by ignoring it.

Nor is it any more comforting or convincing to do as the ardent humanist, Dick Gross, suggests. He writes: 'Fear and denial won't go away, but they can be managed with the right techniques.'[111] But the body of the loved one – whether at age three or one hundred and three – is still lifeless, maybe even battered and mangled. That is the awful reality. Techniques do not change truth.

As Thomas Gray wrote of the 'inevitable hour': 'The paths of glory lead but to the grave'. This is referring to each one of us. This is supposed to be an age of honesty, when all things are out in the open. However, death is not on the agenda. Nevertheless, it refuses to be ignored. In 1623 John Donne caught the plague, and was contemplating his own death as he listened to the bells which signified another death. It was then that he wrote his famous words: 'No man is an island . . . Any man's death diminishes me, because I am involved in Mankinde; and therefore never send to know for whom the bell tolls; it tolls for thee.' One of the most obvious things which unites all humanity is the fact of our common mortality. We all die. That is why Donne kept a skull on his desk – to remind him of his own mortality.

Death is a terror, a horror. It is not nothing or a negligible accident. We do not simply slip next door. Euphemisms only cover the truth for a time. The truth is that death devastates

---

[111] Cited in D. Gross, *Godless Gospel* p. 167.

everything on earth. Emily Dickinson describes the impact of a death in the family:[112]

> *The Bustle in a House*
> *The Morning after Death*
> *Is solemnest of industries*
> *Enacted upon Earth –*
>
> *The Sweeping up the Heart*
> *And putting Love away*
> *We shall not want to use again*
> *Until Eternity.*

Someone has gone, and something is gone. There is emptiness, loss, sorrow, and even anger deep inside us.

The person without God only has this life to live, or so he thinks. This leads to the philosophy that it is better to be a living dog than a dead lion. Better to be a dirty, horrible despised creature that is alive than a noble creature, a picture of kingship, that is dead. Life may be a meaningless farce but it is better than the alternative. A Princeton University student in 1978 carried a poster which read: 'Nothing is worth dying for.'[113] On that view of life, the only reason for pressing on is that the alternative seems worse. The words of Christ sound like dreams from another world: 'For whoever would save his life will lose it, but whoever loses his life for my sake will find it' (*Matt.* 16:25).

Take God out of the equation, and you end up with the views of Jean-Paul Sartre: 'If God does not exist . . . man is in

---

[112] R. W. Franklin (ed), *The Poems of Emily Dickinson* (Massachusetts: Belknap Press, 1999), no. 1108, p. 448.

[113] Cited in Charles Colson with Ellen Santilli Vaughn, *Against the Night* (London: Hodder & Stoughton, 1990), pp. 32–33.

consequence forlorn, for he cannot find anything to depend upon, either within or outside himself.'[114] Ironic – the philosopher believes that life is fundamentally irrational. Not surprisingly, Sartre was never able to live consistently with his views. You and I have to face the fact that death hovers over us all. You will die, you will cease breathing, and all your earthly relationships will come to an end. We must face that. Death is, as Paul says, the last enemy (*1 Cor.* 15:26).

The problem of death is obvious to us all, but also unwelcome. Can you and I solve this one? We may jog around the block each day, eat carrots and zucchinis every meal, and stay off the cigarettes. All of that is good for us, but we still die. I once umpired a squash match where one player, in his forties, walked off the court, sat in a chair, and simply fell over dead. We cannot escape death. When World War 2 broke out, C. S. Lewis commented, 'We now have less chance of dying of Cancer.'[115]

Moses wrote about 1450 B.C. but we all still relate to his words, 'The years of our life are seventy, or even by reason of strength eighty; yet their span is but toil and trouble; they are soon gone, and we fly away' (*Psa.* 90:10). Moses' successor, Joshua, likewise faced the hard facts of life and death. As he neared death, he told his fellow Israelites: 'I am about to go the way of all the earth' (*Josh.* 23:14). Thomas Hobbes' famous description of life was that it is 'nasty, brutish, and short'. We cannot prevent our own deaths. I have a key ring, inscribed with the words 'Eat Right, Exercise, Die Anyway'. It is not the sort of slogan you will find on the wall of your local health club, but it has a certain ring of truth about it.

[114] Cited in Colin Chapman, *The Case for Christianity* p. 18.
[115] Cited in Terry Lindvall, *Surprised by Laughter* p. 272.

Frank Sinatra was famous for singing 'I did it my way', but they were not his words on his deathbed. His last recorded words were: 'I am losing.'

We do not know what to do with death. If there is a minute's silence called on account of the death of some esteemed person, we fidget and inwardly glance about, and find it hard to concentrate our minds. This is because we do not want to meditate deeply on the subject. Our own mortality hurts too much.

William Grimshaw was an Anglican clergyman before he became a Christian. Once he felt his own terrible inadequacy in dealing with death when he tried to counsel a couple whose infant daughter had just died. All he could say to the grieving parents was: 'Put away all gloomy thoughts, and go into merry company and divert yourselves, and all will soon be right.'[116] It is a common response. Do not think about it. Pretend that it will not happen, and get on with life. But the nagging doubts must remain.

The *Histories* of Herodotus record that on one occasion, King Xerxes of Persia reviewed his army, before holding a rowing match which the Phoenicians of Sidon won. Xerxes was enjoying himself, and congratulated himself as a lucky man. But not long afterwards, his uncle, Artabanus, found Xerxes weeping, and asked him the reason. Xerxes replied: 'I was thinking and it came into my mind how pitifully short human life is – for of all these thousands of men not one will be alive in a hundred years' time.' That is the human condition. The only way Xerxes could cope with it was to tell his uncle: 'Let us put aside these gloomy reflections, for we

---

[116] Faith Cook, *William Grimshaw of Haworth* (Edinburgh: Banner of Truth, 1997), p. 19.

have pleasant things in hand.'[117] That is how most people down through the ages have coped with those fleeting intrusions of insight into the human condition.

By the middle of the first century, the Roman emperors were deified at their deaths. Vespasian, who reigned from A.D. 69 to 79, joked on his death-bed: 'Oh dear! I think I am turning into a god.' Domitian, who reigned from A.D. 81 to 96, was rather more serious about the issue, and insisted on being addressed as 'Lord and God'. One could scarcely imagine a more bizarre scenario. To cope with death, the emperors turned reality on its head – that which proves our mortality was declared to prove their divinity.

In the Christian gospel, it is Christ's resurrection which is the greatest proof of his deity. This, of course, is as it should be, and is in harmony with reason and sound thought. John Bacon was a sculptor and a Christian. On his epitaph, he had these words inscribed: 'What I was as an artist seemed to me of some importance while I lived; but what I really was as a believer in Jesus Christ is the only thing of importance to me now.' If Christ did not die for sinners and rise from the dead, the Christian gospel is finished, and we have nothing to say to the world. This is our hope, that Christ died for our sins, that he was buried and that on the third day he rose again for our justification. That is a stupendous claim, not said of Buddha, Mohammed or anybody else. But it is a vital part of the Christian gospel.

What does the claim of resurrection mean for you? You know that you will die. You fear death. As Woody Allen put it: 'I don't want to achieve immortality through my work. I

---

[117] Herodotus, *The Histories*, trans. by Aubrey de Sélincourt, revised by A. R. Burn, (Harmondsworth: Penguin, 1976), p. 461.

want to achieve it through not dying.' But you cannot *not* die. A funeral home sent me a brochure that proclaimed: 'To live in hearts we leave behind is not to die.' But sentimentality is no substitute for truth. You will die.

Death will strike down our loved ones, and it will strike us down too. I have written this, you are reading it, but your life and mine will end in death. Many think that this only means that we will rot in our graves. Others hope against all hope that we will be reincarnated in some other form. But God says that we will be resurrected to face his judgment (*Acts* 17:31; *Heb.* 9:27).

For the one who trusts in Jesus Christ, this is good news, for Christ has paid the price for sin and has conquered death. Christ alone has power over death – he lays down his life that he may take it again (*John* 10:17–18); he calls himself the resurrection and the life (*John* 11:25); he is the first and the last, and lives forevermore (*Rev.* 1:17–18). No other person in history has made such claims, nor has had such claims made for him.

Life is not just futility upon futility. In Christ there is all that we need – forgiveness, power, meaning, and life everlasting. He is offering all that to each one of us even now. Sure, there are real consolations in this life, and there are worthy things we can strive for, and these are in no way to be despised. But death hangs over everything we do – and over our very beings. Your inability to deal with this points to the one who alone can bring life out of death. In fact, he has already done so!

# 11

# The Conclusion
# of the Matter – Almost!

Richard Baxter stated what now seems obvious: 'The more the world is known, the less it satisfieth.' Even the patriarch Jacob lamented to Pharaoh: 'Few and evil have been the days of my life' (*Gen.* 47:9). This world passes away (*1 John* 2:17) – this is a truth written in Scripture and confirmed by all our experience of life.

The Bible has what at first sight seems to be a strange invitation: 'Come, everyone who thirsts, come to the waters; and he who has no money, come, buy and eat! Come, buy wine and milk without money and without price' (*Isa.* 55:1). The invitation does not refer to literal water and literal wine and milk. This is a call to drink from 'the wells of salvation' (*Isa.* 12:3). Hold a glass of water before a man who has just drunk one and hold a glass of water before a man who is hot and sweaty after working for hours in the heat of the day, and you get two different responses. It is the same with the gospel invitation. Only those who realize their need will respond. As Joseph Hart put it:

> *Let not conscience make you linger,*
> *Nor of fitness fondly dream;*

*All the fitness He requireth,*
*Is to feel your need of Him;*
*This He gives you;*
*'Tis the Spirit's rising beam.*

Do you know your need? Or do you still cling to dreams of your supposed self-sufficiency?

Calvin once commented on how difficult it was in his day to make people see their need of God. We have the same problem today. 'The Spirit and the Bride say, "Come." And let the one who hears say, "Come." And let the one who is thirsty come; let the one who desires take the water of life without price' (*Rev.* 22:17). 'Here, drink freely of the wells of salvation' is the invitation. 'Who's thirsty?' is the common response. But if you have followed the message of Ecclesiastes, and looked into the needs of your own heart and conscience, you will have seen the need of God's help by now.

You have sought satisfaction and life in wisdom, pleasure, work, political activities, and the other things of this world, but have only found limited satisfaction. Any sense of achievement has quickly worn off. God has a question for you: 'Why do you spend your money for that which is not bread, and your labour for that which does not satisfy?' (*Isa.* 55:2a). Apart from God, we live like Sisyphus (the legendary king of Corinth) who spent his life in Hades rolling a stone uphill, only to see it roll down again.

You want security, significance, and love – but you, like the rest of us, are all too prone to look for these things in the wrong places. Jesus once spoke to a Samaritan woman by the well of Sychar. He spoke to her of living water which would satisfy her thirst forever. She professed interest, but was surely mistaken when she replied: 'Sir, give me this water, so that I will not be thirsty or have to come here to draw water' (see John 4:10–14). Later, Jesus told his disciples: 'Do not labour for the food that perishes, but for the food that endures to eternal life, which the Son of Man will give to you. For on him God the Father has set his seal' (John 6:27). Down through the ages, people have persisted in trying to find satisfaction in money, pleasure, alcohol, drugs, sex, or achievements of one kind or another.

We live in a society which ultimately says that nothing matters because death is the end, but God tells us that everything matters because death is not the end. After death comes resurrection and judgment. This life is about dealing with that truth.

In Ecclesiastes there is the repeated message that every-thing is ultimately pointless – not just pleasure or laziness but even wisdom and hard work and human achievements. Life fails to deliver what we hoped it would. The best that Albert Camus could suggest is: 'He who despairs of events is a coward, but he who puts his hope in the human condition is a madman.'[118] An understandable conclusion, but can we go any further than that?

Everybody wants to be fulfilled today, but most do not know how to be fulfilled. C. S. Lewis wrote: 'It is when I turn to Christ, when I give myself up to his personality, that I first begin to have a real personality of my own.'[119] It is sin which makes us identical and conformist. We begin to understand ourselves when we realize that to find ourselves means to find

---

[118] Cited in M. A. Casey, *Meaninglessness: The Solutions of Nietzsche, Freud and Rorty* (North Melbourne: Freedom Publishing Co, 2001), p. xv.
[119] C. S. Lewis, *Mere Christianity*, p. 187.

out that we are sinners. The solution to this dilemma must come from outside. It has arrived in the coming of Jesus Christ. He gives meaning and direction in place of futility and vanity.

This world bears the marks of its original creation in God's goodness, and it bears the marks of its rebellious fallenness. John Henry Newman declared that 'the world is sweet to the lips, but bitter to the taste. It pleases at first, but not at last. It looks gay on the outside, but evil and misery lie concealed within.'[120] In different senses, the Christian both loves and hates the world. The world is God's world and so is to be loved as his gift; but it also a wayward and rebellious world and so is to be shunned as his enemy. Bonhoeffer made a vital point when he wrote, 'Only life from God is the goal and the fulfilment, overcoming the contradiction between what is and what should be.'[121]

At the end of the book of Ecclesiastes, Qoheleth is quite emphatic: 'The end of the matter; all has been heard' (*Eccles.* 12:13a). 'The end (or conclusion) of the matter'. Notice how there is no verb in the sentence. Qoheleth is being deliberately abrupt in order to add emphasis. This is what the whole book is about; this is what life is about, this is the sum of all that concerns us. On Camus' tombstone are the words from *The Myth of Sisyphus*: 'The struggle toward the summit itself suffices to fill a man's heart.'[122] Alas, it does not. A ride on the merry-go-round is never as satisfying as arriving at the seashore.

---

[120] Cited in A. R. Vidler, *The Church in an Age of Revolution* (Harmondsworth: Penguin, 1971), p. 278.

[121] Dietrich Bonhoeffer, *My Soul Finds Rest: Reflections on the Psalms*, p. 86.

[122] Cited in Os Guinness, *Long Journey Home*, p. 95.

Ecclesiastes is saying not only that faith will help you to live, but that without God, life is pointless and futile. Before we confront the issue of life after death, we need to ask whether there is life before death. It is as Kierkegaard said: 'In the present age, one is either lost in the dizziness of unending abstraction or saved forever in the reality of religion.'[123]

The alternative to faith in the God of the Bible is grim indeed – it is ultimate futility and meaninglessness, with only a few compensations to keep you going. You get to the top and there is nothing there. In fact, the alternative is so grim that the only way you can cope with it is not to think about it. Instead, we watch television, collect matchbox covers, and play the Lotto. Or, if we have the money of Walt Disney, we have our bodies frozen in the hope that somehow, somewhere science will be able to bring them back to life. But the dream of the ageless youth of Peter Pan has a way of becoming more like the nightmare of the Immortals or Struldbruggs in Jonathan Swift's *Gulliver's Travels* – ever ageing and wishing for death. Qoheleth, in contrast to all worldly hopes, is forcing us to think about reality.

It is realistic to remember that old age is coming – we hope! Youth is short-lived: 'Light is sweet, and it is pleasant for the eyes to see the sun. So if a person lives many years, let him rejoice in them all; but let him remember that the days of darkness will be many. All that comes is vanity. Rejoice, O young man, in your youth, and let your heart cheer you in the days of your youth. Walk in the ways of your heart and the sight of your eyes. But know that for all these things God will bring you into judgment. Remove vexation from your

---

[123] See Soren Kierkegaard, *The Present Age*, trans. by Alexander Dru, (New York: Harper Torchbooks, 1962), p. 81.

[94]

heart, and put away pain from your body, for youth and the dawn of life are vanity' (*Eccles.* 11:7–10).

Your youthful years are behind you before you know it. Yet although youth might be vanity, old age is worse. It is one of the characteristics of old age that the speaker often comments on how quickly time flies. After twenty-five, it is all downhill: 'Remember also your Creator in the days of your youth, before the evil days come and the years draw near of which you will say, "I have no pleasure in them"; before the sun and the light and the moon and the stars are darkened and the clouds return after the rain, in the day when the keepers of the house tremble, and the strong men are bent, and the grinders cease because they are few, and those who look through the windows are dimmed, and the doors on the street are shut – when the sound of the grinding is low, and one rises up at the sound of a bird, and all the daughters of song are brought low – they are afraid also of what is high, and terrors are in the way; the almond tree blossoms, the grasshopper drags itself along, and desire fails because man is going to his eternal home, and the mourners go about the streets' (*Eccles.* 12:1–5). Yes, how swiftly old age and its associated evils come upon us!

The adage that 'youth is for pleasure, maturity for business, and old age for religion' is as fallacious as it is dangerous. Qoheleth describes those who are flagging in energy. The age of cataracts and false teeth is looming. We are like the miner in the song:

> *You load sixteen tons, and what do you get?*
> *Another day older and deeper in debt.*

The great Scottish preacher, Thomas Boston, lost two front teeth in 1724, and this marred the pronunciation of his words. He died on 20 May 1732, having preached his last two sermons, while very ill, from a window in the manse. It is all right to say that you are only as old as you feel, but that sounds like a restatement of the problem, not a prescription of the solution. A positive mind cannot stop the ravages of time. The hearing gets weaker, but a bird wakes you up. Energy runs lower, and one recovers more slowly from injuries. Tremper Longman III translates 'desire' (ESV, NIV, NKJV) in Ecclesiastes 12:5 as 'caper berry' which, he says, is an aphrodisiac, but it is now useless.

There is no fountain of eternal youth on this earth. You go to the school reunion, and you are surprised how old all your schoolmates have become. It is sad how the years have treated them. Not so with you, although you have got to the stage where your idea of a good night is to stay at home. The squash competition starts tomorrow night, but your elbow is still giving you trouble, and both ankles are suspect.

Old age is one thing, but at the end of old age – assuming you survive that long – is death. The silver cord is snapped, the gold bowl is broken, the pitcher is shattered at the fountain, the wheel is broken at the cistern. The dust returns to the earth, and the spirit returns to God who gave it. Vanity of vanities! Temporary of temporaries! Everything is ephemeral (*Eccles.* 12:6–8). Qoheleth is saying nothing about the life to come here. He is simply referring to death as death. You may avoid sickness and suffering in this life. That is unlikely, but it might possibly happen. Yet you cannot avoid death. At its best this life is like a sumptuous feast given to a condemned prisoner. The meal may be quite delicious, and the prisoner may enjoy it, but a terrible foreboding hangs over it all. Eating, drinking, sport, study, going out on the town, entertainment – whatever you enjoy will diminish, and finally be extinguished.

What if God should say to you, as he said to the rich man in Jesus' parable: 'Fool! This night your soul is required of you'? (*Luke* 12:20). The fool was a fool not because he was rich but because he forgot God and he forgot about death. You cannot live life until you have faced the fact of death. Otherwise you are wining and dining on the *Titanic*. There is a huge difference between Paradise and a fool's paradise. It is useless for governments to pass legislation against death or for scientists to promise that a cure may be coming. Death is written into the warp and woof of this fallen world.

The received wisdom that youth is a time for sowing your wild oats and living it up does not make much sense now, does it? There is nothing modern about such an outlook on life – we can see it there in the prodigal son (*Luke* 15:11–32). It is surely wise to remember your Creator in the days of your youth, before the onset of old age with all its attendant problems (*Eccles.* 12:1). One should not overdo this, for Bethan Lloyd-Jones speaks movingly of the 'elderly babes' at Sandfields who were converted when they had more years behind them than in front of them.[124] Nevertheless, it is usually difficult to deal with God and the issues of eternity when your mind is going and you are in pain. People think that they will turn to God before they die, but life is rarely as tidy as that. They may have had a stroke and are now too preoccupied with their physical troubles to give much thought to eternity. That is what happens.

'Remember now' – while you are still coherent enough to read a book like this – the one who created you, and the one who will judge you. 'Fear God and keep his commandments,

---

[124] See Bethan Lloyd-Jones, *Memories of Sandfields 1927–1938* (Edinburgh: Banner of Truth, 1983), pp. 11, 85.

for this is the whole duty of man. For God will bring every deed into judgment, with every secret thing, whether good or evil' (*Eccles.* 12:13b–14).

Fear God and obey him – that is what life is all about. These words are hard words, goads, like well-driven nails, but they are from the 'Shepherd' (*Eccles.* 12:11). They hurt but are for our good. Those who only have soft words for you are not necessarily serving your best interests. Nobody objects if you grab someone or shout at someone who is about to step over a cliff. This is a spur, a barb, a necessary goad given to us by the good Shepherd. God is wonderful, and the alternative is terrible. God is life; the alternative is misery, futility, and death.

Ecclesiastes shows us what life is like for those without faith but who contemplate life. As he grew older, Sir Desmond MacCarthy would lie in very hot baths and repeat over and over again: 'My life, my life.' Meanwhile Cyril Connolly would suck the sheets on his bed, and groan: 'Poor Cyril.'[125] That is the result of trying to gain life out of this dying world. It promises pleasure, but it brings despair.

The unbeliever seeks for pleasure, wealth or wisdom, and gains only a few consolations in a largely meaningless world. The believer finds meaning and coherence in the midst of the Fall – there is a God who judges, and there will be a day of reckoning when all shall be put right.

Perhaps a yet more graphic illustration of the two options that are before you can be seen in the lives and deaths of two men – Horace Greeley and John Wesley. Horace Greeley was editor of the New York *Tribune* from 1841 to 1872. He

---

[125] The accounts of MacCarthy and Connolly are in Jeremy Lewis, *Cyril Connolly: A Life* (London: Pimlico, 1998), p. 157.

believed that man could ennoble himself by his own goodness, and he went on one crusade after another. First, he favoured communes, but they failed; then he wanted a return to the land, then he conducted a crusade against rents. His wife crusaded against the killing of animals for any reason. Believing that human beings are born noble, they raised their son in complete freedom, and did not even cut his hair. He ended up a spoiled brat, but died early. Then they advocated free love, which led to more bondage and misery. Finally on 29 November 1872 Greeley died. This is one of his last statements: 'I stand naked before my God, the most utterly, hopelessly wretched and undone of all who ever lived. I have done more harm and wrong than any man who ever saw the light of day. And yet I take God to witness that I have never intended to injure or harm anyone. But this is no excuse.'[126] All his life, Greeley opposed the Christian faith, and supported one lunatic cause after another. The result was wretchedness and futility unto death. At least he had the honesty and perception to say so. That is one option.

A contrast to the life and death of Horace Greeley was the life and death of John Wesley. Wesley spent his life on horseback, travelling around Britain, seeking, in his own words, 'to reform the nation, particularly the Church, and to spread Scriptural holiness over the land.'[127] He died in 1791. As he was dying, he was asked what he would say. He replied: 'There is no way into the holiest, but by the blood of Jesus.'[128]

---

[126] See Marvin Olasky, *Prodigal Press* (Illinois: Crossway Books, 1988), pp. 45–47.

[127] A. Skevington Wood, *The Burning Heart* (Exeter: Paternoster, 1976), p. 74.

[128] Iain Murray, *Wesley and Men Who Followed* (Edinburgh: Banner of Truth, 2003), p. 97.

Then he sang two verses of Isaac Watts' hymn, *I'll praise my Maker while I've breath*. Then he cried out: 'The best of all, God is with us!' He tried to sing again, but all he could get out was 'I'll praise, I'll praise.'[129] So he died – exactly as he had lived.

How would you like to live and die – like Greeley or like Wesley?

Augustine began his *Confessions* with the sentence: 'You have made us for Yourself, and our hearts are restless till they find their rest in You.' That is the message of Ecclesiastes. Life without God is ultimately futile and meaningless. Sin and death bring all wisdom, pleasure, wealth and work to a grinding halt. It is as the hymn-writer put it,

> *Now none but Christ can satisfy,*
> *None other Name for me!*
> *There's love, and life, and lasting joy,*
> *Lord Jesus, found in Thee.*

There has only been one in history who has overcome sin and death, and that one is Jesus Christ.

---

[129] John Pollock, *John Wesley, 1703–1791* (London: Hodder & Stoughton, 1989), pp. 251–252.

# 12

# Eternity and Madness:
# Both Sides Again

The eternal question, 'How shall I live in order to lead a good life?', has recently been raised again by A. C. Grayling. His answer is decidedly secular and opposed to any form of religion. He lauds those who have put their trust in humanity, and cites Pico della Mirandola, who in his *Oration on the Dignity of Man* in 1486, declared that man has the potential to become anything that he desires.[130] All that we have looked at thus far tells us that such a hope is but a tragic delusion.

As a youth, Asahel Nettleton had never been outwardly wild or extravagant in his unconverted days, but one day he watched the sun go down, and the thought that everyone would die caused him to stand and weep.[131] In 1800, during Connecticut's Second Great Awakening, he came to see his need of regeneration, but also rebelled against this. This new seriousness with regard to his salvation came about not after

[130] A. C. Grayling, *What is Good?* (London: Phoenix, 2004), pp. 104–105.
[131] For Nettleton, see the accounts of Bennet Tyler and Andrew Bonar, *The Life and Labours of Asahel Nettleton* (Edinburgh: Banner of Truth, reprinted 1975); and J. F. Thornbury, *God Sent Revival* (Durham: Evangelical Press, 1988).

a sermon, as is sometimes said, but after he had attended a ball, and found that all his happiness and amusement were overtaken by gloom, with thoughts of death, judgment and eternity.

Nettleton entered a kind of spiritual torture chamber. He wrote: 'I searched the Scriptures daily, hoping to find inconsistencies in them, to condemn the Bible, because it was against me; and while I was diligently pursuing my purpose, everything I read, and every sermon I heard, con-demned me. Christian conversation gave me the most painful sensations.' All his experience testified to the Christian view of total depravity: 'I tried to repent, but I could not feel the least sorrow for my innumerable sins . . . All self-righteousness failed me; and, having no confidence in God, I was left in deep despondency.'

Nothing gave Nettleton any relief. He saw his own wretchedness and the justice of God. Then: 'Eternity – the word *Eternity* – sounded louder than any voice I ever heard; and every moment of time seemed more valuable than all the wealth of the world.'[132] He came to love the character of God, to see the preciousness of the Saviour, and to delight in spiritual meetings and duties. For about ten months, Nettleton had struggled with God and his own soul, and even after that remained cautious about his own spiritual con-dition. The deceitfulness of the human heart appalled him, and so he wrote: 'But my unfaithfulness often makes me fear my sincerity; and should I at last be raised to glory, all the praise will be to God for the exhibition of his sovereign grace.' Nevertheless, as he himself was converted, so he also

---

[132] Bennet Tyler and Andrew Bonar, *The Life and Labours of Asahel Nettleton* p. 22.

preached and lived. Eternity was his salvation – both the means and the goal.

We can deal with the longings for eternity in our hearts when we can deal with the reality of the madness in our hearts. In 1816 Robert Haldane began teaching the book of Romans to about 20–30 divinity students in Geneva. The great historian, Merle d'Aubigné, was one of those students. He recorded: 'I met Robert Haldane and heard him read from an English Bible a chapter from Romans about the natural corruption of man, a doctrine of which I had never before heard. In fact I was quite astonished to hear of man being corrupt by nature. I remember saying to Mr Haldane, "Now I see that doctrine in the Bible." "Yes" he replied, "but do you see it in your heart?" That was but a simple question, yet it came home to my conscience. It was the sword of the Spirit: and from that time I saw that my heart was corrupted, and knew from the Word of God that I can be saved by grace alone.'[133]

To understand life we must understand that we have eternity and madness in our hearts. That is our starting point. Without God, we lose our sense of decency, our capacity for reason, and our reason for living. History is littered with people who, like Felix before the Apostle Paul, put off thinking about these issues until there was supposedly a more convenient time (*Acts* 24:25). You know that there will never be a more convenient time. If you understand the issues, you understand the urgency. The time is now.

Joni Mitchell looked at life from both sides, and sang that she really didn't know life at all. There was nothing to

---

[133] J. H. Merle d'Aubigné, *The Reformation in England, Vol. 1* ed. by S. M. Houghton (Edinburgh: Banner of Truth, reprinted 1971), p. 5.

integrate life, to pull it all together, and to make sense of its many enigmas. By grace, we can go further than that. We cannot know everything, but we can know life in Christ. Nobody understood our perilous, yet still hopeful, condition better than Blaise Pascal. He saw that 'it is equally dangerous for man to know God without knowing his own wretchedness as to know his own wretchedness without knowing the Redeemer who can cure him . . . Jesus Christ is the object of all things, the centre towards which all things tend. Whoever knows him knows the reason for everything . . . but it is not possible to know Christ without knowing both God and our wretchedness alike.'[134]

[134] Blaise Pascal, *Pensées* pp. 167–169.

*Also available from the
Banner of Truth Trust:*

# The Pundit's Folly
### Chronicles of an Empty Life
### SINCLAIR B. FERGUSON

'The Bible is by no means a predictable book . . . The book of Ecclesiastes definitely comes into the "surprising" and "unpredictable" category. After all, you would hardly expect a book of the Bible to begin with the words "Meaningless! Meaningless! says the Teacher. Utterly meaningless! Everything is meaningless!" Nor would you expect to find: "Man's fate is like that of the animals; the same fate awaits them both: As one dies, so dies the other. All have the same breath; man has no advantage over the animal. Everything is meaningless."

'So, who is this "Teacher" and what is his message? One thing seems obvious – he has tapped into the despair that many people experience. But he also has more positive things to say – the book demonstrates the profound hope that Ecclesiastes holds out to us today. Sinclair Ferguson has written this very helpful, easy-to-read book which leads you through the message of Ecclesiastes and explains the fascinating story of why the author wrote it and what hope he offers for the emptiness of our own generation.'

EVANGELICAL TIMES

ISBN 0 85151 676 9
96 pp., paperback

# Ecclesiastes

## CHARLES BRIDGES

Of the older writings on Ecclesiastes, this commentary by Charles Bridges, a Christian leader of the nineteenth century, stands out. Bridges believed that the book could be fully understood and applied only in the light of the gospel of Christ. He found an abundance of spiritual lessons in Ecclesiastes and used them to provide food for the souls of his readers. The commentary consists of short portions which are suitable for use as daily readings.

'There can be no more relevant message for our day than the message of Ecclesiastes – that the things which attract and delight us in this present evil world are all vanity, and that our true happiness consists in the enjoyment and service of God.'

EVANGELICAL MAGAZINE OF WALES

ISBN 0 85151 322 0
352 pp., clothbound

*For free illustrated catalogue please write to*

THE BANNER OF TRUTH TRUST

3 Murrayfield Road,      P O Box 621, Carlisle,
Edinburgh EH12 6EL      Philadelphia 17013,
UK                                    USA